# STUDIES IN ENGLISH LITERATURE No. 64

*General Editor*

David Daiches

Professor of English in the School of English
and American Studies, University of Sussex

## Already published in the series:

# Already published in the series (*continued*):

# POETRY OF THE
# FIRST WORLD WAR

by

J. M. GREGSON

EDWARD ARNOLD

First published 1976 by
Edward Arnold (Publishers) Ltd.
25 Hill Street, London W1X8LL

ISBN cloth: 0 7131 5930 8
paper: 0 7131 5931 6

To Eddy Harrison
an unlikely source of inspiration
when he least suspected or expected it

*Printed in Great Britain by*
*The Camelot Press Ltd, Southampton*

# General Preface

The object of this series is to provide studies of individual novels, plays and groups of poems and essays which are known to be widely read by students. The emphasis is on clarification and evaluation; biographical and historical facts, while they may be discussed when they throw light on particular elements in a writer's work, are generally subordinated to critical discussion. What kind of work is this? What exactly goes on here? How good is this work, and why? These are the questions that each writer will try to answer.

It should be emphasized that these studies are written on the assumption that the reader has already read carefully the work discussed. The objective is not to enable students to deliver opinions about works they have not read, nor is it to provide ready-made ideas to be applied to works that have been read. In one sense all critical interpretation can be regarded as foisting opinions on readers, but to accept this is to deny the advantages of any sort of critical discussion directed at students or indeed at anybody else. The aim of these studies is to provide what Coleridge called in another context 'aids to reflection' about the works discussed. The interpretations are offered as suggestive rather than as definitive, in the hope of stimulating the reader into developing further his own insights. This is after all the function of all critical discourse among sensible people.

Because of the interest which this kind of study has aroused, it has been decided to extend it first from merely English literature to include also some selected works of American literature and now further to include selected works in English by Commonwealth writers. The criterion will remain that the book studied is important in itself and is widely read by students.

DAVID DAICHES

# Contents

# Acknowledgements

The publishers' thanks are due to the following for permission to reproduce copyright material: G. T. Sassoon for extracts from the poems of Siegfried Sassoon; the Owen Estate and Chatto & Windus Ltd for extracts from Wilfred Owen's poems which appeared in *The Collected Poems of Wilfred Owen* © Chatto & Windus Ltd (1946), © 1963, reprinted by permission of New Directions Publishing Corporation, New York; Schocken Books Inc. and Chatto & Windus for extracts from *Collected Poems of Isaac Rosenberg* and Mr Robert Graves for six lines from his poem 'Dead Boche'.

# 1. Rupert Brooke and the Initial Reaction

'A scribbled message was thrown across the screen: "War declared with Austria, 11.9." There was a volley of quick low handclapping—more a signal of recognition than anything else. Then we dispersed into Trafalgar Square, and bought midnight war editions, special. All these days I have not been so near tears. There was such tragedy, and such dignity, in the people.'

(*The Prose of Rupert Brooke*)[1]

Thus Rupert Brooke described his own and the British public's reaction to the outbreak of war. The reaction was carried forward into the initial months of the war and into Brooke's war sonnets, by far the most famous and influential of the early war writing. Probably no poems have been so acclaimed and so disparaged within the space of one generation as these five sonnets. Brooke's already established reputation as poet and scholar, his remarkable physical grace and beauty, his death and the publicizing of his poems at a moment of immense psychological significance, combined to make him a figure of almost mythical significance in the popular imagination. Frances Cornford's famous epigram on the young Brooke, written in his undergraduate days, was the stuff on which legends are built:

> A young Apollo, golden-haired,
> Stands dreaming on the verge of strife,
> Magnificently unprepared
> For the long littleness of life.

His death seemed in the atmosphere of early 1915 a ritual sacrifice of one

[1] Full details of abbreviated titles will be found in the bibliography, together with those of critical works not footnoted in the text.

of the nation's finest sons as evidence of the justice of the moral crusade on which England was felt to have embarked. Mass emotion is not the atmosphere in which incisive critical evaluation flourishes; between the extremes of reaction to Brooke's war poems there is usually a gap of several years.

Winston Churchill's famous obituary of Brooke was written in terms of eulogy which helped to consolidate the position of Brooke's war poems:

> . . . this life has closed at the moment when it seemed to have reached its springtime. A voice had become audible, a note had been struck, more true, more thrilling, more able to do justice to the nobility of our youth in arms engaged in this present war, than any other—more able to express their thoughts of self-surrender, and with a power to carry comfort to those who watched them so intently from afar. The voice has been swiftly stilled. Only the echoes and the memory remain; but they will linger.
>
> (*The Times*, 26 April 1915)

Later and less spontaneous reactions to Brooke have been less generous. F. R. Leavis[2] condemned his work as 'the vulgarity of Keats with a public-school accent' and V. de S. Pinto, writing in 1951, dismissed him thus:

> He was a wonderfully accomplished versifier in the manner that was orthodox among the pundits of the public school culture of his day, but his mind remained to the end that of a clever public schoolboy.

It is easy to see why Brooke secured such a remarkable reputation following his championing by Churchill and Dean Inge, who as Dean of St Paul's, quoted and eulogised 'The Soldier' in his Easter sermon of 1915, in St Paul's Cathedral. Though the sonnets were written in November and December and published in December 1914, there had been no immediate response. But Brooke's romantic death (actually from blood-poisoning, but in circumstances which were deliberately left vague by Churchill and others to imply a death in action) and the publicity accorded to his work in the months which followed secured his posthumous success. *1914 and Other Poems* was published in June 1915 and this and his collected poems sold 300,000 copies over the next decade.

[2] Quoted by Pinto, p. 150.

In sweet-sounding, easily understood lines with a fine ring and cadence, Brooke caught the national mood of resolution and elation in a conflict that was seen in prospect as clear-cut, swift and heroic. It is significant that it was Churchill who, responding sincerely to Brooke's sonnets, saw at the same time their possibilities as an elevated call to a united nation. A quarter of a century later, Churchill was to seize the mass medium of radio and, in his memorable series of broadcasts commencing in 1940, to unite a nation at home and in arms in a unique resolution. Before the immediacy of the spoken word was possible as a form of mass communication, Brooke came nearest to capturing the feeling of the nation as a whole in the early years of the Great War, at once voicing and forming the spirit of resolution as Churchill was to do in the later context. If the resolution was to be misused and eventually perverted that is not Brooke's fault. If in retrospect rhetoric is the most powerful note sounded in Brooke's sonnet sequence, it was released upon a public eager for such rhetoric.

Nor did the response to Brooke come only from the unthinking, the unread or those alert to his value as an evangelist of the war. Fellow-writers are usually more generous than eminent critics, even when they have the benefits of hindsight, and Sir Herbert Read[3] reminds us in *Annals of Innocence and Experience* that:

> It must be remembered that in 1914 our conception of war was completely unreal. We had childish memories of the Boer War, and from these and from a general confusion of Kiplingesque sentiments, we managed to infuse into war a decided element of adventurous romance. War still appealed to the imagination.

Edmund Blunden wrote that:

> Few of those who were in the early phase of war service as Brooke was in 1914 and 1915 and heard his 'music' will ever have forgotten it, even though they might survive into years of deepening despair and horror which for them made its graces unsuitable.[4]

As Kitchener's face pointed accusingly from every hoarding and Brooke was writing 'Now God be thanked who has matched us with His hour' the recruits poured in. Kitchener asked for only an initial 100,000. In fact 175,000 volunteered in the single week ending 5 September 1914

[3] See Ford, p. 165.      [4] *War Poets 1914–18*, pp. 16–17.

and 750,000 had enlisted by the end of September. Then the average ran at 125,000 a month until June 1915 when it slackened off; in all two and a half million men enlisted before conscription was introduced in March 1916.[5]

Brooke's poetry, then, at once reflected and exalted the feelings of the hour. How are we to weigh it as poetry half a century later? It is necessary to consider briefly Brooke's pre-war poetry and the ideas it reflects if we are to understand the literary content of the war sonnets. Rupert Brooke, perhaps by virtue of his own energy, personality and influence as much as his literary stature, was one of the leaders of that group of poets known as the Georgians, who took themselves very seriously as innovators of a new school of poetry, but who now appear merely as a group of minor poets occupying one of the lesser literary culs-de-sac. In an excellent introduction to a selection of Georgian poetry published in the sixties,[6] James Reeves summarizes its virtues as 'natural simplicity, emotional warmth and moral innocence', and its most usual faults as 'technical slackness—the use of imprecise diction and facile rhythm; sentimentality of outlook; trivial, and even downright commonplace, themes'.

This is hardly a formidable catalogue of poetic equipment or experience with which to tackle the cataclysm which befell the world in 1914. One of Brooke's difficulties is simply that his previous experience of life and poetic experiment had not prepared him to write about the brutalities of war in explicit terms. Unfortunately for his poetic reputation he was not given the time and the fighting experience to change his attitude to the war and to modify or discard the techniques with which he expressed his first reaction. Others, such as Sassoon and Owen, were more fortunate.

Two qualities in Brooke's earlier poetry should be mentioned since they are clearly present in the war sonnets. The first is a preoccupation with death. It is this disenchantment with life which makes him willingly embrace war as a heroic purposeful variant to his own rather aimless life, and a soldier's death as an honourable escape.

Death is a theme of all five of the war sonnets and two of them are actually titled 'The Dead'. One of these begins with characteristic Georgian versification and language:

[5] Figures from A. J. P. Taylor, *English History, 1914–45*, O.U.P., 1965, p. 20.
[6] *Georgian Poetry*, 1962.

These hearts were woven of human joys and cares,
Washed marvellously with sorrow, swift to mirth.
The years had given them kindness. Dawn was theirs,
And sunset, and the colours of the earth.

The inappropriateness of the Georgian approach for the theme of war is obvious in retrospect. Neither Brooke nor his contemporaries were aware of the impending clash of theme and techniques at the time he wrote his sonnets, and it took experience of the Western front to underline the paradox with full harshness.

The second element in Brooke's work which should be underlined is his facility for sound effects of great beauty, an apparent poetic strength which is also a potential weakness, as the war-sonnets were to illustrate. When the technique is applied without discrimination to the theme of death in war it produces a quiet slow rhythm and a series of falling cadences which give the sonnets an effective dignity of sound when read aloud. Thus the sonnet on the dead, the opening lines of which I have quoted above, ends with the sestet:

There are waters blown by changing winds to laughter
And lit by the rich skies, all day. And after,
Frost, with a gesture, stays the waves that dance
And wandering loveliness. He leaves a white
Unbroken glory, a gathered radiance,
A width, a shining peace, under the night.

Any investigation of the sense rather than the sound of these lines diminishes their impact. The image of frost stilling the happy laughter into a state of deep-frozen peace is curious and incompletely worked out. For those unhappy with life, the mere cessation of existence may be an attractive idea. To dress up this negative satisfaction as something more profound and attractive is a piece of self-deceit which would be more instantly recognizable as such were it not for Brooke's skilled manipulation of sound-effects. His death-wish and his too readily indulged talent for verse-music lead him in this sonnet into an intellectual vacuum. The only connection with war is that the war seems to Brooke to provide an honourable outlet from life and thus a starting-point for the sentiments expressed.

The other 1914 sonnets enshrine more effectively the reactions to the war of Brooke and the millions of others involved in the initial enthusiasm. Brooke, because of his fame, has received most of the critical brickbats of later generations, but there were many less noble and less poetically meritorious calls to arms than his. None then thought it presumptuous that those without experience of front-line fighting should write about the war, since almost all war poetry before 1914, including the most famous pieces such as Tennyson's 'Light Brigade', was written by poets without direct experience of the incidents described. Thus Henry Newbolt, fifty-two when the war began, could pen his famous lines about public school leadership:

> There's a breathless hush in the Close tonight—
> Ten to make and the match to win—
> A bumping pitch and a blinding light,
> An hour to play and the last man in. . . .

> The river of death has brimmed his banks,
> And England's far, and Honour a name,
> But the voice of a schoolboy rallies the ranks:
> 'Play up! play up! and play the game!
> (*Vitai Lampada.*)

Nor was this the worst; William Watson's 'Sons of Britain' might make some such perverse claim:

> Sons of her who keeps her faith unbroken,
> Her who gave you might of limb and nerve
> Her whose service—be it devoutly spoken—
> Perfect freedom is, for all who serve. . . .

> Heed not overmuch when she is slandered;
> Yours to guard her from a bully's blow:
> Yours to rise, and rally to her standard:
> Yours to arm, and face the brutal foe.

This drivel is not worth detailed comment, but lest it be thought it was regarded with appropriate levity at the time, it is worth recalling that both Newbolt (in 1915) and Watson (in 1917) were knighted for their patriotic and propaganda verse; Sassoon's anger at the kind of war-picture being presented to civilians in 1916 and 1917 is easy to comprehend when one reads such verses, most of them of course now mercifully out of print. Virtually every newspaper carried recruiting poems of the same kind as Watson's throughout the later months of 1914. Against this background, Brooke's sonnets have a nobility of sound and a note of integrity which are immediately striking:

> Now, God be thanked Who has matched us with His hour,
> And caught our youth, and wakened us from sleeping,
> With hand made sure, clear eye, and sharpened power,
> To turn, as swimmers into cleanness leaping,
> Glad from a world grown old and cold and weary,
> Leave the sick hearts that honour could not move,
> And half-men, and their dirty songs and dreary,
> And all the little emptiness of love!

This first war sonnet has a fine ring and a single telling image—'as swimmers into cleanness leaping'—but again sound is sometimes exploited at the expense of sense. Are the three epithets 'old', 'cold' and 'weary' the most accurate for the poet's dismissal of the pre-war world, or are they chosen primarily for the cumulative sound effect of their long syllables? The best poets of course—and among war poets Owen is pre-eminent in this respect—use sound effects to reinforce sense, starting always from sense so that meaning is heightened and reinforced by the sound effects rather than subservient to them. As an expression of world-weary lassitude and a ready response to a new, potentially heroic, personal situation, the sonnet has some effect. If one is to take the poem as reflecting something more generalized than a personal feeling, one is bound to ask questions about the dismissal of the 'half-men, and their dirty songs and dreary' and of 'all the little emptiness of love'.

The sonnet is typical of its time in its unquestioning acceptance of the hand of God in the war, on the British side of course. It is typical also of Brooke's slender output of war poems in that the predominant impression is one of emotion. V. de S. Pinto remarks that Brooke's war sonnets are poems which are managed by mass emotions as opposed to poems such as those of Hardy on the South African war where the poetry controls the emotion.[7] There is much in this, though it is probably an overstatement. Brooke's emotion is not out of control, for he uses poetic techniques of versification and cadence to full effect to convey that emotion. What happens is that the heart rules the head to such an extent

[7] *Crisis in English Poetry*, p. 157.

that intellect is always a poor second to emotion, and is readily sacrificed when the two conflict. Thus the sonnet concludes with a glad acceptance of the 'supreme sacrifice' that never confronts the ugly reality of death in war:

> Oh! we, who have known shame, we have found release
>     there,
> Where there's no ill, no grief, but sleep has mending,
> Naught broken save this body, lost but breath;
> Nothing to shake the laughing heart's long peace there
> But only agony, and that has ending;
> And the worst friend and enemy is but Death.
>
> *(Peace)*

The second war sonnet, 'Safety', celebrates in sonorous bardic lines the notion that death in this honourable war is the surest guarantee of safety. Again the emotion sings, the cadences fall, the ideas are not investigated beyond their surface attraction.

It was of course an emotional time and the initial enthusiasm now looks like mass hysteria. One would be doing Brooke less than justice if one did not point out that other men, many of them now more highly esteemed poets than Brooke, were greeting the war with similar excited emotion. Siegfried Sassoon, whose reputation rests on the vivid bitter anger he made into memorable war poetry from 1916 onwards, greeted the war in exactly the same poetic strain as Brooke—indeed in direct imitation of him:

> The anguish of the earth absolves our eyes
> Till beauty shines in all that we can see.
> War is our scourge; yet war has made us wise,
> And, fighting for our freedom, we are free.
>
> *(Absolution)*

Robert Graves records his first meeting with Sassoon in November 1915:

At this time I was getting my first book of poems, *Over the Brazier*, ready for the press. I had one or two drafts in my pocket-book and showed them to Siegfried. He frowned and said that war should not be written about in such a realistic way. In return, he showed me some of his own poems. One of them began:

> 'Return to greet me, colours that were my joy,
> Not in the woeful crimson of men slain . . .'

Siegfried had not yet been in the trenches. I told him, in my old soldier manner, that he would soon change his style.[8]

This laconic verdict on Sassoon's early war verse would have been as applicable to Brooke and his output.

Even Wilfred Owen was writing lines in 1914 which expressed the same sentiments as Brooke's but which lacked at that stage his mastery of sound-effects and verse-patterns. The ballad form in which Owen attempted to treat this high theme results in something very like doggerel:

> O meet it is and passing sweet
> To live in peace with others,
> But sweeter still and far more meet
> To die in war for others.
> *(Ballad of Purchase Money)*

That this sentiment is so devastatingly demolished three years later in 'Dulce et Decorum Est' only underlines what Brooke might have achieved had he too been spared for front line experience. For again it took trench fighting to mature Owen's work. If one examines the pre-1914 output of the war poets who have won greater critical acclaim than Brooke in after years—of Blunden, Graves, Sassoon and Owen for example—there is little evidence that they were technically in advance of Brooke, and if they were thinking more deeply and more constructively than he, it is scantily reflected in their poetic output. Indeed, it is often forgotten that Brooke was something of a poetic rebel, albeit a rather self-conscious one. Edward Marsh certainly had some difficulty in keeping him within the confines he thought appropriate for Georgian poetry.

There is some evidence in Brooke's pre-war poetry of a willingness to experiment with unpleasant themes and of a technique which might have been adapted to deal with them effectively; it is slender evidence, but scarcely more slender than any in the work of the poets named above. In 'Dawn' he shows he can treat other themes than escapist ones and show the sharp observation and selection of detail which are to be the war poet's stock-in-trade:

[8] *Goodbye to All That*, p. 146.

> Opposite me two Germans snore and sweat.
> Through sullen swirling gloom we jolt and roar.
> We have been here for ever: even yet
> A dim watch tells two hours, two aeons, more.
> The windows are tight-shut and slimy-wet
> With a night's foetor. There are two hours more;
> Two hours to dawn and Milan; two hours yet.

There is evidence here of a willingness to turn his mastery of sound-effects to more varied purpose, to make it the poet's servant rather than his master; to vary the characteristic verse and rhyme schemes of the Georgians for different effects in themes demanding greater realism; to use more varied and irregular rhythms with conscious control for particular poetic purposes. The poem went largely unremarked at the time, and seems to have been an experiment on Brooke's part, but this is a voice well capable of adaptation to the reality of war after experience.

And yet, when all has been said, what might have been is a matter for the sentimentalist, the biographer, and possibly the historian, but not the literary critic. However explicable seem Brooke's sentiments when he is set in his historical and literary context, whatever the hints of a potential which he was not allowed to realize, our concern here must finally be with the war poetry he left and not with the hypothetical output which might have been his had he lived. If the benefits of hindsight lead to a more brutal verdict, it is the function of the critic to apply just such hindsight with full severity. Such analysis reveals important deficiencies as well as the virtues already remarked: both are well illustrated in the most famous of his 1914 sonnets, which are the only two not so far considered in detail, the third one, 'The Dead' and the fifth, 'The Soldier'.

The first of these reveals a considerable mastery of the sonnet form as well as the usual melodic persuasion:

> Blow out, you bugles, over the rich Dead!
> There's none of these so lonely and poor of old,
> But, dying, has made us rarer gifts than gold.
> These laid the world away; poured out the red
> Sweet wine of youth; gave up the years to be
> Of work and joy, and that unhoped serene,

That men call age; and those who would have been,
Their sons, they gave, their immortality.

Blow, bugles, blow! They brought us, for our dearth,
Holiness, lacked so long, and Love, and Pain.
Honour has come back, as a king, to earth,
And paid his subjects with a royal wage;
And Nobleness walks in our ways again;
And we have come into our heritage.

Brooke's capacity to produce a heightened effect by his understanding of verse techniques and of the possibilities and the limitations of the sonnet-form has too seldom been remarked. The long syllables and falling cadences echo the obvious starting-point of the sonnet, the last post. The use of ever vaguer and grander (to the modern reader grandiose) abstractions—from the dead he moves to youth, age, immortality, holiness, honour and nobleness—give a consistency of effect which is typical of the most telling use of the sonnet-form.

The sonnet has often been criticized on the grounds that it does not make sense. This is patently unfair. The idea of the blood shed in war as 'the sweet wine of youth' and the conceit of the dead giving up their tangible link with posterity because they died before siring offspring, 'those who would have been', are perfectly clear, even if rather high-flown. What critics really mean is that they do not like the ideas expressed because they seem superficial or naïve. This they certainly are. There is a failure to consider whether this war is such an overwhelming moral crusade that it offers the kind of heroic martyrdom postulated. There is also a refusal to confront the reality of death, not only in this war but in any war. Brooke seems to have seized the opportunity of the war to project the private poetic preoccupation with death noted earlier into a generalized context. His talent for melodic invention has led him to a bardic celebration of death, a piece of self-delusion which was adopted by a contemporary readership looking for just such delusion. Despite the obvious care with which the lines have been turned and the sound effects worked out, the final effect of the sense of the poem is one of intellectual self-indulgence.

Some of Owen's early war efforts display, as well as more subtle intellectual questioning, an awareness that the poetic techniques fashionable in the immediate pre-war years were not going to be adequate for the new material of war. Thus his first poem about the war, the sonnet entitled in one draft '1914' and in another 'The Seed', is even further from the war and ends in even vaguer abstractions, couched in less effective verse-music, than Brooke's, but shows much more resolution to confront the intellectual implications of war:

> War broke: and now the Winter of the world
> With perishing great darkness closes in.
> The foul tornado, centred at Berlin,
> Is over all the width of Europe whirled,
> Rending the sails of progress.

Already Owen apprehends the war not as the romantic crusade but as an international catastrophe, 'the winter of the world'. Owen is the most interesting comparison with Brooke, for he it is who shows how Brooke's sensitivity to sensuous images and melodic effects may be combined with greater intellectual rigour and front-line experience of the war to produce more profound and moving poetry. Thus in 'Greater Love' he combines the lyric strain and deep emotion with a passionate intellectual complexity and harnesses the gentle sexual images of conventional love poetry with the violent images of war:

> Red lips are not so red
>     As the stained stones kissed by the English dead.
> Kindness of wooed and wooer
> Seems shame to their love pure.
> O Love, your eyes lose lure
>     When I behold eyes blinded in my stead!
>
> Your slender attitude
>     Trembles not exquisite like limbs knife-skewed,
> Rolling and rolling there
> Where God seems not to care;
> Till fierce love they bear
>     Cramps them in death's extreme decrepitude.

The interest of this is that it is in some respects very near to Brooke: the essential addition is an intellectual one.

The most famous and most anthologized of all Brooke's 1914 sonnets is 'The Soldier', still probably one of the half-dozen best-known poems in our language. It begins:

> If I should die, think only this of me:
> That there's some corner of a foreign field
> That is for ever England. There shall be
> In that rich earth a richer dust concealed;
> A dust whom England bore, shaped, made aware,
> Gave, once, her flowers to love, her ways to roam,
> A body of England's, breathing English air,
> Washed by the rivers, blest by suns of home.

Certainly this caught the feeling of the hour: C. E. Montague in 'Disenchantment' argues that 'the plain recruit who had not the gift of style "said to himself in his own way exactly the same thing about the immortal hour as Brooke was saying more eloquently here".[9] As Edmund Blunden points out, it is not Brooke's fault if the poem later came to be regarded and was actually used as 'not so much a great poem as a great piece of war propaganda'. Again the line of argument is more consistent than some commentators have given Brooke credit for, but it is the schoolboy stance of the *Boy's Own Paper* and of a score of Henty novels now long out of print. There is no hint of the internationalism one might expect of an acclaimed scholar in the sincere but thoughtless egotism of 'In that rich earth a richer dust concealed'.

The sestet of the sonnet has more serious, and by now more familiar, Brookean defects:

> And think, this heart, all evil shed away,
> A pulse in the eternal mind, no less
> Gives somewhere back the thoughts by England given;
> Her sights and sounds; dreams happy as her day;
> And laughter, learnt of friends; and gentleness,
> In hearts at peace under an English heaven.

Again Brooke retreats into a curiously amorphous after-life which certainly does not reflect the conventional Christian ethic: it is ironic that Dean Inge should have chosen this sonnet to extol from the pulpit of St Paul's. There is a spurious mysticism about the notion that the treasures listed earlier are to be given back 'somewhere' to England. The truth is that Brooke is once again beguiled by his preoccupation with sound effects and desire to convey what is to him the vague but overwhelmingly attractive idea of peace in death. This leads to lines that for all their highly

[9] See Blunden, *War Poets*, p. 18.

polished effect are ultimately self-indulgent and lacking in poetic detachment.

Had Brooke lived, his '1914' sonnets would have provided an interesting starting point; as it is they are often treated as his definitive statement on war. Their chief value in a study of war poetry lies not in their poetic quality or in depth of thought and feeling but in their summary of the spirit of the time.

In a fragment that Brooke wrote on the troopship just before his death in 1915 there is evidence that he is aware that there is a need for a new, more sober style, and that the search for it has begun:

> I strayed about the deck, an hour, tonight
> Under a cloudy moonless sky; and peeped
> In at the windows, watched my friends at table,
> Or playing cards, or standing in the doorway,
> Or coming out into the darkness. Still
> No one could see me.
>
>                I would have thought of them
> —Heedless, within a week of battle—in pity,
> Pride in their strength and in the weight and firmness
> And link'd beauty of bodies, and pity that
> This gay machine of splendour'ld soon be broken,
> Thought little of, pashed, scattered.
>
>                                    (Fragment)

It is a slight piece, and presumably without benefit of revision, but in its discarding of rhyme and solemn music, its conversational ease, there is a very different tone from that of the 1914 sonnets.

The final verdict on Brooke's war sonnets must be that they are fatally marred by a cerebral deficiency. This is what I. A. Richards meant when he said that Brooke's poetry 'had no inside'.[10] Edward Thomas wrote of Brooke in a letter to Robert Frost:

> . . . thought gave him (and me) indigestion. He couldn't mix his thought or the result of it with his feeling. He could only think about his feeling.[11]

When all qualifications have been made, this remains a fitting comment on the war sonnets.

---

[10] See Pinto, p. 159.          [11] J. Silkin, *Out of Battle*, p. 68.

## 2. Charles Sorley and the First Hints of Realism

> I regard the war as one between sisters, between Martha and Mary, the efficient and intolerant against the casual and sympathetic. Each side has a virtue for which it is fighting, and each that virtue's supplementary vice.
>
> (Letters of Charles Sorley)

Thus did Charles Sorley, barely nineteen, announce an unusually independent spirit and a detachment almost unique among those who rushed to enlist in the early weeks of the war. It is the more remarkable for being penned as Brooke planned his euphoric war sonnets and tales were spread by civilian propagandists of Germans cutting off the heads of Belgian babies. In any history of the literature of the war, Sorley occupies a place of peculiar interest as the first voice consistently sounding the notes which are to be expanded into an insistent chorus during the last two years of the war. He has more to offer, however, than a message steadily and bravely in advance of his time; the poetic merits of his tiny contribution are of greater importance than his place in the chronology of war writing.

Born in Aberdeen in 1895, Sorley enjoyed the same kind of privileged background as most of the war poets. His father was a professor of Philosophy at Cambridge, and Charles was educated at Marlborough. His school poems are largely the juvenilia common to many of the war poets at this stage, though his 'Song of the Ungirt Runners' has been much anthologized. His mind, however, had developed an early maturity and a sturdy determination to question false logic and patriotic platitudes, as his letters, some of the most intriguing and liveliest of the period, constantly reveal. Instead of going to Cambridge at the conclusion of his

Marlborough career, Sorley went to study in Germany in January 1914, remaining there until 2 August, when he returned to enlist in the Suffolk Regiment later that month. After training, he saw some four and a half months of action, rising to the rank of Captain before he was killed in action on 13 October 1915, on the last day of the Battle of Loos, the first great bloodbath of the war.

In one of the best studies of the literature of the Great War,[1] Bernard Bergonzi maintains that 'the collapse of the patriotic myth-patterns of 1914–15 left all the best poets of the time disorientated and in search of a more valid frame of reference.' As a generalization this is true, and there is no doubt that experience at the front was the most powerful single element in shaping this new framework. Yet Sorley's work shows him as perceptive of the poetic as of the philosophical situation. He wrote:

> The voice of our poets and men of letters is finely trained and sweet to hear; it teems with sharp saws and rich sentiment; it is a marvel of delicate technique: it pleases, it flatters, it charms, it soothes: it is a living lie.
>
> (*Letters of Charles Sorley*)

Most remarkably in view of his age, it was Sorley in a letter of April 1914, who anticipated the verdict on Brooke's war poems which a later generation was to arrive at in a less emotional atmosphere:

> . . . He is far too obsessed with his own sacrifice, regarding the going to war of himself (and others) as a highly intense, remarkable and sacrificial exploit, whereas it is merely the conduct demanded of him (and others) by the turn of circumstances, where non-compliance with this demand would have made life intolerable. It was not that 'they' gave up anything of that list he gives in one sonnet: but that the essence of these things had been endangered by circumstances over which he had no control, and he must fight to recapture them. He has clothed his attitude in fine words: but he has taken the sentimental attitude.
>
> (*Letters of Charles Sorley*)

These views are of interest in considering one of Sorley's best-known early war poems, 'All the Hills and Vales Along'. The opening lines suggest the steady marching rhythms characteristic of many efforts early in the war by young poets exultant with the physical energy of military

[1] *Heroes' Twilight.*

manoeuvres and optimistic about the outcome (the poem has an alternative title of 'Route March'):

> All the hills and vales along
> Earth is bursting into song,
> And the singers are the chaps
> Who are going to die perhaps.

The predominant influence on the style of the poem is Housman, but after this opening verse there are persistent subtleties and ambivalences which denote deep thought about the coming issues and the search for a new voice to express them. Thus in the second verse Sorley, beginning in the same tone he set in the first verse, suddenly breaks the rhythm and the sense completely with a harsh aside in lines 4 to 6 which foreshadows the post-war techniques of Yeats or Eliot:

> Cast away regret and rue,
> Think what they are marching to,
> Little give, great pass.
> Jesus Christ and Barabbas
> Were found the same day.
> This died, that went his way.

Where Brooke saw the earth as friendly and consoling,

> There shall be
> In that rich earth a richer dust concealed
> > (*The Soldier*)

and even Owen was to offer as consolation in death the thought of being

> one with nature, herb and stone,
> > ('*A Terre*')

Sorley uses images that show earth as indifferent or hostile and point a savagely ironic contrast between what the poet says and the uncomplicated marching rhythm in which he says it:

> Teeming earth will surely store
> All the gladness that you pour.
>
> Earth that never doubts nor fears,
> Earth that knows of death, not tears,

> Earth that bore with joyful ease
> Hemlock for Socrates,
> Earth that blossomed and was glad
> 'Neath the cross that Christ had,
> Shall rejoice and blossom too
> When the bullet reaches you.

The last verse of the poem is an apparently exultant Housmanesque evocation of optimistically marching troops but the subtleties already noted in the two earlier verses prepare us for the deliberately ambivalent and flat conclusion:

> Strew your gladness on earth's bed,
> So be merry, so be dead.

One of the respects in which Sorley foreshadows a later era of poetry is the way in which he combines and at his best fuses diverse, even contradictory experiences and different poetic styles. As Bergonzi points out, 'Rightly or wrongly, "complex" has become a major term of approbation in present-day criticism. . . . In this respect Sorley's poems are complex, lacking the singlemindedness of Brooke or Grenfell.' 'All the Hills and Vales Along' is an example of this deliberate complexity and the challenge to the reader which it implies; most of his other war verse exhibits some element of the same challenge.

Sorley wrote home in a letter enclosing some of his poems:

> You will notice that most of what I have written is as hurried and angular as the handwriting: written out at different times and dirty with my pocket: but I have had no time for the final touch nor seem likely to have for some time.

*(Letters of Charles Sorley)*

Sometimes this is evident in his work, though it is difficult to know how much inconsistency is due to the experimentation proper to a young poet searching for a new voice and how much to the exigencies of trench conditions. Of two sonnets on 'Death' dated 12 June 1915, the second is so different in tone and technique that it suggests deliberate contrast. The flat low-key opening of the poem suggests in both style and content a direct reply to Brooke's sonnets, Sorley's condemnation of which some six weeks earlier has already been noted:

> Such, such is Death: no triumph: no defeat:
>     Only an empty pail, a slate rubbed clean,
>     A merciful putting away of what has been.
>
> And this we know: Death is not Life effete,
>     Life crushed, the broken pail. We who have seen
>     So marvellous things know well the end not yet.

Sorely continues with broken rhythms emphasizing the untidiness of death, and a resolute dismissal of Brookean verse-music:

> Victor and vanquished are a-one in death:
>     Coward and brave: friend, foe. Ghosts do not say
> 'Come, what was your record when you drew breath?'
>     But a big blot has hid each yesterday
> So poor, so manifestly incomplete.

Sorley's refusal to join in the anti-German hysteria has already been noted, and his arrival at the front only sharpened this stance in everyday conditions.

He penned a remarkable sonnet, 'To Germany'. It is at once prophetic of thoughts of poets much later in the war and a triumph of the new techniques Sorley is working out. The opening octet combines constantly changing verse-rhythms, direct and simple, almost conversational language, and mastery of rhyme to produce a remarkable effect, and one new not only in the poetry of the war but in poetry in general:

> You are blind like us. Your hurt no man designed,
> And no man claimed the conquest of your land.
> But gropers both through fields of thoughts confined
> We stumble and we do not understand.
> You only saw your future bigly planned,
> And we, the tapering paths of our own mind,
> And in each other's dearest ways we stand,
> And hiss and hate. And the blind fight the blind.

The intellectual compression of this and the logical development of the argument through the poetic vehicle to the burning simplicity of the conclusion of the argument in the last line are its most impressive qualities; they are an extreme contrast with Brooke's intellectual slackness and convoluted language. Of course, there are inconsistencies in the output of a young poet writing under trench conditions. His epitaph on a friend, though couched in simpler terms, is based on sentiments as unquestioning about the war as Brooke's:

> There is no fitter end than this.
>   No need is now to yearn nor sigh.
> We know the glory that is his,
>   A glory that can never die.
>       (*In Memoriam S.C.W., V.C.*)

The reason why the poem is oddly out of tune with Sorley's other front-line output is probably that he is not reacting to the general war situation, as he is in his best work, where he conveys a resolutely independent reaction and philosophy in the new poetic techniques he is exploring. His response to the horrors of the war is interesting in this respect. Robert Graves, the other major poet to react as early as this to front-line experience, is able to shock with the horrors of detail which are to become familiar ingredients of war poetry from this point onwards:

> Where, propped against a shattered trunk,
> In a great mess of things unclean,
> Sat a dead Boche; he scowled and stunk
> With clothes and face a sodden green,
> Big-bellied, spectacled, crop-haired,
> Dribbling black blood from nose and beard.
>
> > (*Dead Boche*)

The horror is explicit and the poem serves its primary purpose of shocking the reader, but beyond this Graves is able to do little with the experience; the poem remains an effectively vivid description of a detail of war. Sorley seems to draw more general issues from the plethora of suffering about him. Thus the despair and frustration of being tiny parts of a huge machine manipulated in a meaningless and inhuman way, feelings that are commonplace in 1917 and 1918, are recognized early by Sorley, and caught in memorable lines:

> A hundred thousand million mites we go
> Wheeling and tacking o'er the eternal plain,
> Some black with death—and some are white with woe.
> Who sent us forth? Who takes us home again?

The picture of vast armies moving ant-like over western Europe is etched with vivid compression in the first two lines of this. Sorley's now familiar technique of a sudden breaking of verse rhythms in the third and fourth lines is an effective device for his bitterly despairing questions.

Even the explicit pictures of death and suffering call forth a different response from Sorley than from Graves and his many followers. There is an interesting contrast between Sorley's reaction to these elements in his letters and the way he chooses to use the experience in his poetry. In a letter of August 1915 he writes in explicit terms of the brutalizing effect of night patrols:

> Rustling of the grasses and grave-tapping of distant workers: the tension and silence of encounter, when one struggles in the dark for moral victory over the enemy patrol: the wail of the exploded bomb and the animal cries of wounded men. Then death and the horrible thankfulness when one sees that the next man is dead: 'We won't have to *carry* him in under fire, thank God; dragging will do': hauling in of the great resistless body in the dark, the smashed head rattling: the relief, the relief that the thing has ceased to groan: that the bullet or bomb that made the man an animal has now made the animal a corpse. One is hardened by now: purged of all false pity: perhaps more selfish than before. The spiritual and the animal get so much more sharply divided in hours of encounter, taking possession of the body by swift turns.
>
> (*Letters of Charles Sorley*)

This is a description similar to those found in a dozen memoirs written after the war and hundreds of poems written in the last two years of the war, though the conclusion reveals Sorley's characteristic intellectual complexity and determination to explore ideas to their conclusion, qualities which make him so effective a contrast to Brooke and a forerunner of Rosenberg. The interesting point is that in his poetry he eschews such explicit and detailed horror and searches for a generalized reaction. In one of his most famous poems, the sonnet usually known by its opening line, Sorley confronts the bleakness of death with characteristic honesty and vision:

> When you see millions of the mouthless dead
> Across your dreams in pale battalions go,

Say not soft things as other men have said,
That you'll remember. For you need not so.
Give them not praise. For, deaf, how should they know
It is not curses heaped on each gashed head?
Nor tears. The blind eyes see not your tears flow.
Nor honour. It is easy to be dead.

The fact that the sentiments of this sonnet are so different from those of Brooke on the same theme has often diverted commentators from full consideration of the poetic merits of the Sorley piece. Thus while the third line is probably a direct reference to Brooke, it has an integral place within the framework of the poem. The Keats-like sound effect of this line is contrasted with the uncompromising note of the next, which is emphasized by the abrupt break in rhythm in mid-line. The simplicity of the language may be a contrast to Brooke's artificiality but it is also the appropriate vehicle for the rejection of the conventional glorifying of the dead. This reaches its climax in the bleak line of monosyllables,

Nor tears. The blind eyes see not your tears flow

preparing us for the flat conclusion of this line of argument in the next line,

It is easy to be dead.

The natural line of development of Graves and his followers is into the savage ironies of Sassoon. Sorley's link is with the larger war issues which form the concern of Rosenberg and of Owen's greatest work. But in his intellectual questioning, his deliberate ambivalence, his yoking together of apparently disparate ideas and techniques, Sorley foreshadows the post-war developments in poetry. His is an astonishing achievement for one who was barely twenty when he died.

# 3. Siegfried Sassoon: Disillusion and Anger

I am making this statement as an act of wilful defiance of military authority, because I believe that the war is being deliberately prolonged by those who have the power to end it.

I am a soldier convinced that I am acting on behalf of soldiers. I believe that this war, upon which I entered as a war of defence and liberation, has now beome a war of aggression and conquest. . . . I have seen and endured the sufferings of the troops, and I can no longer be a party to prolong those sufferings for ends which I believe to be evil and unjust. . . .

July 1917. S. Sassoon (*Statement to Commanding Officer*)

The terms in which Siegfried Sassoon's now famous protest against the war was couched are a key not only to his own character but to his poetry. In all his best work, his target is clearly identified and his aim sure. He is the supreme propagandist among the war poets, as sharp, as concentrated, as bitter as any lampoonist or satirical cartoonist.

Because he enlisted on 3 August 1914, saw prolonged service at the front, and survived the war, Sassoon is the best barometer of the evolving emotional responses to the war made by the fighting men. If Brooke caught the mood of 1914—and inspired Sassoon among others to imitation—then Sassoon's vivid angry tirade speaks for the fighting men of 1917 and 1918.

Reference has already been made in the first chapter to Sassoon's early war-verse and the naïvety of its attitude and techniques, and recapitulation of this early phase is unnecessary here. Although Sassoon was actually in uniform on the first morning of the war, it was 1916 before he saw front-line service at Mametz Wood and the Somme; hence Robert Graves' comment on his early war poetry (see pages 14–15), which was soon vigorously confirmed. The change from Sassoon's 1914 attitude:

Now God is in the strife,
And I must seek him there
(*A Mystic as Soldier*)

was swift and dramatic once he became involved in the reality of this
war. The evolution is charted in his first collection of war verse,
published as *The Old Huntsman and Other Poems* in 1917. Already by 'The
Redeemer' in 1916 there is a note of sober reality:

> Darkness: the rain sluiced down; the mire was deep;
> It was past twelve on a mid-winter night,
> When peaceful folk in beds lay snug asleep;
> There, with much work to do before the light,
> We lugged our clay-sucked boots as best we might
> Along the trench; sometimes a bullet sang,
> And droning shells burst with a hollow bang;
> We were soaked, chilled and wretched, every one;
> Darkness; the distant wink of a huge gun.

The reporter's eye which is the basis of all Sassoon's war writing is here at
work: Wordsworth's contention that a principle for any poet should be
'the eye on the object' is nowhere more consistently realized than in
Sassoon's war output. Predominantly among the war poets, Sassoon
reveals his compassion for individual soldiers as a motivating force in his
work. At this stage, he is not directly critical of the conduct of the war,
but the pity for the common soldier's lot which is to drive him so fiercely
to his later protests is already a hallmark. This acute sympathy for his men
as individuals remains with Sassoon throughout his agonies of mind of
1917 and 1918; it is found for instance in one of his last and most moving
fragments of the war, 'The Dug-Out', written in July 1918:

> Why do you lie with your legs ungainly huddled,
> And one arm bent across your sullen, cold,
> Exhausted face? It hurts my heart to watch you,
> Deep-shadow'd from the candle's guttering gold;
> And you wonder why I shake you by the shoulder;
> Drowsy, you mumble and sigh and turn your head. . . .
> *You are too young to fall asleep for ever;*
> *And when you sleep you remind me of the dead.*

As his work developed, Sassoon began to experiment with the language of the ordinary private as well as using his pitiable lot as subject-matter. The first example is 'In the Pink':

> So Davies wrote: 'This leaves me in the pink'.
> Then scrawled his name: 'Your loving sweetheart, Willie'.
> With crosses for a hug. . . .
>
> And then he thought: to-morrow night we trudge
> Up to the trenches, and my boots are rotten.
> Five miles of stodgy clay and freezing sludge,
> And everything but wretchedness forgotten.
> Tonight he's in the pink; but soon he'll die.
> And still the war goes on—*he* don't know why.

At this stage, Sassoon remains predominantly a reporter, able to pin down in words the physical hardship and misery of the soldier's daily life on the western front, but not usually seeking to do more than provide the kind of explicit picture he gives in 'A Working Party':

> Three hours ago he blundered up the trench,
> Sliding and poising, groping with his boots;
> Sometimes he tripped and lurched against the walls
> With hands that pawed the sodden bags of chalk.

In three poems written towards the end of this first phase of his war writing, however, Sassoon speaks in what is to emerge as his character-istic vein. By 1916 there had arisen what V. de S. Pinto has called the division of British society into two nations, the Nation at Home and the Nation Overseas, with a growing cleavage between the two. The Nation at Home still believed in the patriotic myth of the heroic war; the Nation Overseas, in touch with the obscenity of life and death in the trenches, was completely disillusioned about the glorious nature of the struggle. To understand the nature of Sassoon's anger and the role he eventually conceived for himself, it is necessary to remember the diet of rapturous and dishonest prose on which civilians in England, still relatively inexperienced in the uses and abuses of literacy, were fed. Most of it is long out of print: the few examples quoted in this chapter may be of interest in setting Sassoon's poetic stance in context.

The most famous cartoonist of this or any war was Bruce Bairnsfather, whose wry survivors amidst the mud of the Somme and Passchendaele have an enduring truth and humour. Bairnsfather was sent for by the War Office in 1916 and placed in the Intelligence Department as an officer-cartoonist: his book *Bullets and Billets* published in December 1916, sold in great numbers and bears the stamp of an 'official' account:

> We all considered the trenches a pretty rotten outfit; but everyone was prepared to accept far rottener things than that. There was never the least sign of flagging determination in any man there, and I am sure you could say the same on the whole front . . . just think of some poor devil half-way along those corduroy boards struggling with a crate of biscuits; the ration dump behind, the trenches on in front. When he has finished he will step down into the muddy slush of a trench, and take his place with the rest, who, if need be, will go on doing that job for another ten years without thinking of an alternative. The Germans made a vast mistake when they thought they had gauged the British temperament.

Millions of words in this vein were fed to the civilian masses long after the reality of the war had become apparent to the troops in Europe. The increasing note of desperation in Sassoon's determination to open the eyes of those at home is better understood if one recalls this; it leads to some of his best war verse, as in 'Blighters', where he underlines the division between fighting men and others in an apparently united nation. This was one of the last poems in this first group of Sassoon's war poetry, written after a visit to the Liverpool Hippodrome in 1917:

> The House is crammed: tier beyond tier they grin
> And cackle at the Show, while prancing ranks
> Of harlots shrill the chorus, drunk with din;
> 'We're sure the Kaiser loves our dear old Tanks!'
>
> I'd like to see a Tank come down the stalls,
> Lurching to rag-time tunes, or 'Home, sweet Home',
> And there'd be no more jokes in Music-halls
> To mock the riddled corpses round Bapaume.

This is Sassoon at his best and most characteristic: anger, irony and brevity are its chief elements. This and other poems of his have sometimes been accused of being 'not poetry', whatever is meant by that large phrase. On the contrary, Sassoon is completely aware of the poetic devices he is using and deploys them with great exactitude. The harsh consonant sounds and short vowels of the opening lines support the telling choice of words to emphasize the poet's distaste; the facile rhymes of this opening quartet of lines underline the hollow banality of this civilian reaction. The switch to the fighting men in the last line is more than effective propaganda: the pathos of its dying fall of sound and the vividness of the image of the front, suddenly set against the equally vivid tawdriness of the music-hall scene, linger in the mind long after the message has been absorbed.

I pointed out in my first chapter that the Georgians brought to the war a set of techniques which they soon found inadequate to deal with the material which confronted them. Sassoon is interesting in this respect. He showed no originality of verse and metre techniques: most of his poems, like the one above, use the smooth rhymed decasyllables of Georgian lyrics; it is indeed one of the sadder facts of literature that Sassoon lapsed in postwar years into minor verse with an unmistakably Georgian stamp. But Sassoon did contribute more to the development of war poetry than he is usually given credit for. The attempt to write in simple language which could be read by the troops about whom he is writing is an idea which originates with Wordsworth, but which Sassoon arrived at through his burning preoccupation with truth and with the right poetic medium to convey it. The colloquial tone which he uses so effectively has apparent links with Kipling's 'barrack-room ballads', though Sassoon uses it more surely and for very different purposes; this colloquial strain came to Sassoon through Hardy, whose work he much admired (*The Old Huntsman and Other Poems* is dedicated to Hardy), and his talent for accurate reporting led him to use it with increasing subtlety and skill. Finally, Sassoon is the master of the satirist's art of juxtaposition, of yoking together two different ideas or experiences to underline a viewpoint with humour or bitterness. Thus in the poem quoted above he uses the clichés of the bombastic civilians to set against the reality of the war, at once underlining the hollowness of the first and the bitter pathos of the second.

The second short poem which should be noted from *The Old Huntsman* collection is 'The Hero'. This time Sassoon's target is more specific and more hallowed: the wives and mothers of the troops. Robert Graves quotes a 1916 letter from 'A Little Mother' to the *Morning Post* which was

reprinted immediately in pamphlet form and sold 75,000 copies in less
than a week direct from the publishers:

> . . . I say that we women, who demand to be heard, will tolerate no
> such cry as 'Peace! Peace!' where there is no peace. . . . There is only
> one temperature for the women of the British race, and that is white
> heat. With those who disgrace their sacred trust of motherhood we
> have nothing in common. Our ears are not deaf to the cry that is ever
> ascending from the battlefield from men of flesh and blood whose
> indomitable courage is borne to us, so to speak, on every blast of the
> wind. We women pass on the human ammunition of only sons to fill
> up the gaps, so that when the 'common soldier' looks back before
> going 'over the top' he may see the women of the British race at his
> heels, reliable, dependent, uncomplaining. . . .

Sassoon's reaction is swift, accurate and shocking, his anger directed
not at the women but at the system which keeps them in such ignorance
about the war:

### THE HERO

'Jack fell as he'd have wished', the Mother said,
And folded up the letter that she'd read.
'The Colonel writes so nicely'. Something broke
In the tired voice that quavered to a choke.
She half looked up. 'We mothers are so proud
Of our dead soldiers.' Then her face was bowed.

Quietly the Brother Officer went out.
He'd told the poor old dear some gallant lies
That she would nourish all her days, no doubt.
For while he coughed and mumbled, her weak eyes
Had shone with gentle triumph, brimmed with joy,
Because he'd been so brave, her glorious boy.

He'd thought how 'Jack', cold-footed, useless swine,
Had panicked down the trench that night the mine
Went up at Wicked Corner; how he'd tried
To get sent home, and how, at last, he died,
Blown to small bits. And no one seemed to care
Except that lonely woman with white hair.

Again the verse techniques are Georgian, but again Sassoon achieves a new effect. The bathos of the first two verses is underlined by the sudden direct vigour and compression of the last one, with the switch to the colloquial tone of the language of frustrated reality in 'cold-footed useless swine' and the uncompromising simplicity of 'Blown to small bits', its violence pointed by its placing at the beginning of a line and emphasized by the closing return to the 'lonely woman with white hair'.

The third poem of note at the end of this first volume of Sassoon's war writing is 'They'. Here Sassoon has another target; perhaps, as D. J. Enright[1] remarks, rather a sitting one. But again it is difficult for modern readers to appreciate the effect of the Church's support for the war. The note set by Dean Inge's approval of Brooke's 'Soldier' sonnet remained basically that of the hierarchy of the English Church throughout the war. By 1917 Sassoon saw himself as an anti-war propagandist and such an influential opponent as the Church was bound to be demolished; it was the Church at home and its platitudinous non-combatants that excited his greatest anger:

### 'THEY'

> The Bishop tells us: 'When the boys come back
> 'They will not be the same; for they'll have fought
> 'In a just cause: they lead the last attack
> 'On Anti-Christ; their comrades' blood has bought
> 'New right to breed an honourable race,
> 'They have challenged Death and dared him face to face.'
>
> 'We're none of us the same!' the boys reply.
> 'For George lost both his legs; and Bill's stone blind;
> 'Poor Jim's shot through the lungs and like to die;
> 'And Bert's gone syphilitic: you'll not find
> 'A chap who's served that hasn't found *some* change.'
> And the Bishop said: 'The ways of God are strange!'

The techniques which Sassoon is to use to such effect are by this stage fully forged. The high-flown clichés of the bishop are set against the colloquial force of the soldiers' complaints to emphasize both. Again the complaint has been raised that this is hardly poetry but a political cartoon, but art conceals art, and this argument ignores the skill Sassoon has

[1] *Pelican Guide to English Literature*, Volume 7, p. 173.

shown, not only in his selection of details and his ear for speech, but in the way he has absorbed both kinds of talk into the framework of the rhymed decasyllables of his metre. This potentially constricting verse format is used with such fluency that it becomes a major instrument in the ironic effect of the poem.

There is not space here to document the intricacies of Sassoon's protest about the war, initiated by the statement quoted at the outset of this chapter. It must be sufficient to say that Sassoon followed the prolonged display of physical courage which had earned him the nickname of 'Mad Jack' in the trenches with as great a display of moral courage in circumstances which could have led to his court-martial and death, had it not been for the intervention of Robert Graves and others amongst his friends. The importance of the episode for the critic is the reflection of Sassoon's feelings about the war in his second group of war poems, published as *Counter-Attack and Other Poems* in 1918.

A new and insistent note is the brutalizing effect of the war on the men involved in fighting it; in the following extract from 'The Rear-Guard' of April 1917, only the taut parenthesis of the first line explains the soldier's violence and insensitivity:

> 'God blast your neck!' (For days he'd had no sleep,)
> 'Get up and guide me through this stinking place.'
> Savage, he kicked a soft, unanswering heap,
> And flashed his beam across the livid face
> Terribly glaring up, whose eyes yet wore
> Agony dying hard ten days before;
> And fists of fingers clutched a blackening wound.

It has been fairly said that the effect of a mass of such verse is a bludgeoning of the reader's reactions and ultimately a dulling of his receptiveness. In fact, it is a charge more fairly levelled at some of his imitators than at Sassoon himself. While in quantity and consistency of aim *Counter-Attack* is a political pamphlet, there is considerable variety in the way the poet drives home his message. There is verse of the kind just quoted, which Sassoon occasionally deliberately allows to slip from control to a note of near hysteria to underline the urgency of his theme:

> They leave their trenches, going over the top,
> While time ticks blank and busy on their wrists,

> And hope, with furtive eyes and grappling fists,
> Flounders in mud. O Jesus, make it stop!
>
> *(Attack)*

But there are also caricatures of the staff drawn with swift Hogarthian strokes:

> If I were fierce, and bald, and short of breath,
> I'd live with scarlet Majors at the Base,
> And speed glum heroes up the line to death.
> You'd see me with my puffy petulant face,
> Guzzling and gulping in the best hotel,
> Reading the Roll of Honour. 'Poor young chap,'
> I'd say—'I used to know his father well;
> Yes, we've lost heavily in this last scrap.'
> And when the war is done and youth stone dead,
> I'd toddle safely home and die—in bed.
>
> *(Base Details)*

Some of these show Sassoon's talent for absorbing fragments of every-day speech into tightly rhymed metre to achieve an epigrammatic effect:

> 'Good-morning; good-morning!' the General said
> When we met him last week on our way to the line.
> Now the soldiers he smiled at are most of 'em dead,
> And we're cursing his staff for incompetent swine.
> 'He's a cheery old card,' grunted Harry to Jack
> As they slogged up to Arras with rifle and pack
>
> . . . . . . . . .
>
> But he did for them both by his plan of attack.
>
> *(The General)*

And of course Sassoon's contempt for the politicians and propagandists whom he now saw as deliberately prolonging a pointless war grows ever more insistent, reaching its climax in the grim 'Fight to a Finish':

> Snapping their bayonets on to charge the mob,
> Grim Fusiliers broke ranks with glint of steel,
> At last the boys had found a cushy job.
>
> . . . . . . . . .

> I heard the Yellow-Pressman grunt and squeal;
> And with my trusty bombers turned and went
> To clear those Junkers out of Parliament.

Here emotion overcomes detachment, and though the message is stark and clear, the poetic effect is less satisfying than when Sassoon uses more subtle devices. Thus in 'Suicide in the Trenches' he moves in twelve lines from an invocation of the happy warrior in Kiplingesque terms, to the reality of trench existence and death, and finally to the hollowness of the civilian attitude to the war:

> I knew a simple soldier boy
> Who grinned at life in empty joy,
> Slept soundly through the lonesome dark,
> And whistled early with the lark.
>
> In winter trenches, cowed and glum,
> With crumps and lice and lack of rum,
> He put a bullet through his brain.
> No one spoke of him again.
>       . . . . . . . .
> You smug-faced crowds with kindling eye
> Who cheer when soldier lads march by,
> Sneak home and pray you'll never know
> The hell where youth and laughter go.

In 'Glory of Women' he resumes his attack on those particular bastions of the supply of fighting men, female romanticism and ignorance of the reality of the carnage:

> You love us when we're heroes, home on leave,
> Or wounded in a mentionable place.
> You worship decorations; you believe
> That chivalry redeems the war's disgrace.
> You make us shells. You listen with delight,
> By tales of dirt and danger fondly thrilled.
> You crown our distant ardours while we fight,
> And mourn our laurelled memories when we're killed.
> You can't believe that British troops 'retire'
> When hell's last horror breaks them, and they run,

> Trampling the terrible corpses—blind with blood.
>   O German mother dreaming by the fire,
>   While you are knitting socks to send your son
>   His face is trodden deeper in the mud.

The language is straightforward and sober; the rhyme is cleverly devised and varied in the last six lines to emphasize the irony; the significance of the casually inserted *German* mother is particularly telling in conveying the impartiality and senselessness of the Flanders bloodbath. With typical honesty, Sassoon does not spare himself, and the line 'And mourn our laurelled memories when we're killed' is an ironic echo of his own 1915 verse epitaph on his brother which has the line 'But in the gloom I see your laurelled head'.

Perhaps the finest poem in the collection is the ten-line 'Survivors', written at Craiglockart in October 1917 where Sassoon had been sent to recover from the mental breakdown which was eventually determined by an Army Medical Board to be the cause of his protest against the war:

> No doubt they'll soon get well; the shock and strain
>   Have caused their stammering, disconnected talk.
> Of course they're 'longing to go out again',—
>   These boys with old, scared faces, learning to walk.
> They'll soon forget their haunted nights; their cowed
>   Subjection to the ghosts of friends who died,—
> Their dreams that drip with murder; and they'll be proud
>   Of glorious war that shatter'd all their pride. . . .
> Men who went out to battle, grim and glad;
> Children, with eyes that hate you, broken and mad.

The compassion for the suffering and betrayed fighting man is here caught in superb images—the 'boys with old, scared faces', the 'dreams that drip with murder', the 'Children, with eyes that hate you'. Within a succession of these pictures the popular press platitudes are placed to maximum effect, and the rhyme, often yoking together two contrasting ideas, as in the last two lines, is as ever a faithful servant of the poet's intention. This taut compressed little cameo of a particular scene and its implications, with the message more effective for being implicit, is typical of Sassoon at his best.

Sassoon's place in the poetry of the First World War is assured. He lacks the vision, the range of techniques, the profundity and variety of emotion of Owen and Rosenberg, but in narrow and direct effects he is unsurpassed. He turns familiar and unpretentious metres and rhymes and a bitter wit to forceful and ironic effect, and his language is hard, simple and sharply defined. As he desired to be, he is always immediately accessible; his work never contains the associative suggestions of poets of larger resources. Yet he achieved the effects he aimed at in his poetry. In March 1919 he wrote a reminder to the conscience of the world which ended:

> Do you remember the stretcher-cases lurching back
> With dying eyes and lolling heads—those ashen-grey
> Masks of the lads who once were keen and kind and gay?
>
> Have you forgotten yet?. . . .
> Look up, and swear by the green of the spring that you'll
> never forget.
>
> (*Aftermath*)

He as much as anyone has ensured by his war verse that we shall not forget.

# 4. *Wilfred Owen and the Wider Vision of War*

. . . And you have fixed my life—however short. You did not light me: I was always a mad comet; but you have fixed me. I spun round you a satellite for a month, but I shall swing out soon, a dark star in the orbit where you will blaze. It is some consolation to know that Jupiter himself sometimes swims out of ken!

Letter of Wilfred Owen to Siegfried Sassoon,
(*Collected Letters*, p. 504), 5 November 1917

The famous meeting between Sassoon and Owen at Craiglockhart in the autumn of 1917 is well documented, the best account being probably that of Sassoon himself in Chapter 6 of *Siegfried's Journey*. In the year following the letter quoted above, Owen combined the multifarious duties of a platoon officer with an outpouring of poetic intensity which curiously parallels that of his beloved Keats. While his output in this period shows in full measure the independence and originality which are essential elements in any claim to poetic greatness, the key to the understanding of Owen's work lies in the cardinal influences upon him of Keats and of Sassoon. One could scarcely select two more contrasting figures in the varied catalogue of English poets, yet the quality of Owen's poems in his last year is testimony to the effectiveness of their influence and of the poet's ability to harness such contrasting strains with full discrimination.

Owen, although he was eventually commissioned in the Manchester Regiment in June 1916, did not have the same sort of privileged, public-school background as Brooke, Sorley, Sassoon and the majority of the other war poets. Though he attended the Shrewsbury Technical School as a day boy and matriculated at London University at the age of eighteen in 1911, he went to Dunsden vicarage, Oxfordshire, as pupil and lay assistant to the vicar. Though his mother obviously hoped that this would be the first stage in a career in the Church, the experience undermined rather than consolidated the young Wilfred's faith, and he underwent a minor nervous breakdown in the summer of 1913 after relinquishing this post. He spent the next two years tutoring in France, returning to England and enlisting in the Artists' Rifles in October 1915.

Owen is perhaps the most brilliant example of that phenomenon noted throughout this little book, the impact of trench experience upon not only the content but the quality of writing. In introducing the definitive collection of Owen's work published in 1963, C. Day Lewis wrote:

Reading through what survives of the unpublished poetry Owen wrote before 1917, I found myself more and more amazed at the suddenness of his development from a very minor poet to something altogether larger. It was as if, during the weeks of his first tour of duty in the trenches, he came of age emotionally and spiritually. His earlier work . . . is vague, vaporous, subjective, highly 'poetic' in a pseudo-Keatsian way, with Tennysonian and ninety-ish echoes here and there: the verse of a youth in love with the *idea* of poetry.

The story of Owen's evolution as a poet of stature is the story of his learning, not to discard his beloved Keats, but to fuse this strain with gradually increasing discipline with other elements until he spoke with a voice effective for the material with which war confronted him. In this evolution, his meeting with Sassoon played a key part, not least because Owen found himself taken seriously and encouraged by a poet of established stature, as Sassoon by this time was because of his own war verse: it is easily forgotten that only four of Owen's poems were published while he was alive. The impact of war, and in due course, of Sassoon's counsel, on the Keatsian groundwork of Owen's style are of great interest.

In 'Spring Offensive' written in July 1918, he uses his lyrical strain to establish an ironic backcloth to a war incident:

> Marvelling they stood, and watched the long grass swirled
> By the May breeze, murmurous with wasp and midge,
> For though the summer oozed into their veins
> Like an injected drug for their bodies' pains,
> Sharp on their souls hung the imminent line of grass,
> Fearfully flashed the sky's mysterious glass.
>
> Hour after hour they ponder the warm field—
> And the far valley behind, where the buttercup
> Had blessed with gold their slow boots coming up,
> Where even the little brambles would not yield,
> But clutched and clung to them like sorrowing hands;
> They breathe like trees unstirred.

The second and third lines are almost direct echoes from Keats' 'Ode to Autumn', and the whole shows a similar delight and competence in sound effects, but there are enough vivid images, such as the personification of the brambles, to announce an individual talent. The imitation of the nature lyric is in any case direct and deliberate, for Owen uses it as an elaborate ironic scene-setting for the horror and waste which are the real theme of the poem:

> So, soon they topped the hill, and raced together
> Over an open stretch of herb and heather
> Exposed. And instantly the whole sky burned
> With fury against them; earth set sudden cups

>           In thousands for their blood; and the green slope
>           Chasmed and steepened sheer to infinite space.

The Keatsian use of colour is here combined with the nightmare images of the last three lines to produce an effect which is at once vivid and more generalized and abstract than Sassoon's particular horrors. Owen's own nightmares and the neurasthenia which sent him to Craiglockhart are important elements in the poetic material and attitudes of his last year's work. The verse above shows the mastery of the more obvious devices of poetry which Owen revealed only in his later work. After an opening ironic effect, the rhyme which runs through the earlier verses is suddenly abandoned, and the verse rhythms broken into disarray, while words such as 'exposed', 'burned' and 'chasmed' receive emphasis from their placing in positions of maximum stress. However, though the lyric strain is set alongside the reality of war to fine ironic effect in the poem, with each section supplementing the other's effects, word-music and realism are hardly fused as in his best work, and the economy and compression which are keynotes of all great poetry are not as marked as elsewhere.

Although Owen's models did not include the metaphysical poets, in 'Greater Love', already quoted on page 18 he disciplines his sensuous awareness with a passionate intelligence, showing a daring suggestive of Donne. The erotic strain of this, deriving from the love lyrics whose style he is using for angry ironic contrast, shows a willingness to experiment with new poetic approaches to find a voice appropriate for the grim material which surrounded him.

He writes in similar vein, with a Keatsian determination to seek beauty in unlikely places, even of a soldier's mortal wound:

>           I saw his round mouth's crimson deepen as it fell,
>               Like a Sun, in his last deep hour;
>           Watched the magnificent recession of farewell,
>               Clouding, half gleam, half glower,
>           And a last splendour burn the heavens of his cheek.
>               And in his eyes
>           The cold stars lighting, very old and bleak,
>               In different skies.

There is a hint in the last two lines of the cosmic grandeur of Owen's best work, and the probably deliberate ambivalence of the last line prefigures the intellectual complexity of the last poems.

There is also a hint of the patronizing attitude to the uneducated soldier of which Owen is sometimes accused. In the much-praised 'Insensibility' he sees him thus:

> Alive, he is not vital overmuch;
> Dying, not mortal overmuch;
> Nor sad, nor proud,
> Nor curious at all.
> He cannot tell
> Old men's placidity from his.

Owen learned better through his war experience, and in 'Futility' he showed supremely how this sympathy could be combined with his lyric strain while avoiding a descent into sentimentality:

> Move him into the sun—
> Gently its touch awoke him once,
> At home, whispering of fields unsown.
> Always it woke him, even in France,
> Until this morning and this snow.
> If anything might rouse him now
> The kind old sun will know.
>
> Think how it wakes the seeds,—
> Woke, once, the clays of a cold star.
> Are limbs, so dear-achieved, are sides,
> Full-nerved—still warm—too hard to stir?
> Was it for this the clay grew tall?
> —O what made fatuous sunbeams toil
> To break earth's sleep at all?

Owen endured the terrible winter of 1916–17 in the trenches, and the poem obviously derives from an incident during this. But it moves quickly from the particular to the general, even from the world to the universe, from a particular moment in time to prehistory. By reinforcing its final questions with these huge weights of time and place it becomes a more powerful questioning of this war, of all war, of the Christian ethic of the after-life, than Sassoon's agonized 'O Jesus, make it stop!' The poem, too, shows an almost Shakespearean grasp of profundity through simplicity, of deep emotional impact through understress. Owen's most original introduction, consonantal rhyme or para-rhyme, is deployed to great effect, giving the poem a sound unity which emphasizes the development of its thought without the artificiality which full rhyme might impose on the directness of the language used. Despite its apparent simplicity there is a tremendous poetic compression at work here. Lines such as 'Woke, once, the clays of a cold star' and 'Was it for this the clay grew tall?' with their effortless suggestion of elemental forces, show a range and vision greater than those of any war poet except Rosenberg. I. M. Parson's[1] estimate of this short piece as 'one of the great poems to come out of the war, out of any war' seems to me entirely justified.

This poem shows the effects of war experience on Owen's lyric strain. We should realize that even before his meeting with Sassoon, the impact of war was apparent in Owen's work. 'Exposure', written early in 1917, shows a Keatsian apprehension of sound and vision applied to war material through the vehicle of a more direct style:

> Our brains ache, in the merciless iced east winds that knive us . . .
> Wearied we keep awake because the night is silent . . .
> Low, drooping flares confuse our memory of the salient . . .
> Worried by silence, sentries whisper, curious, nervous,
>     But nothing happens.

The poem's close is uncompromising, chilling not only in the realism of its picture but in its implicit assumption of the indifference of the Almighty:

> Tonight, His frost will fasten on this mud and us,
> Shrivelling many hands, puckering foreheads crisp.
> The burying-party, picks and shovels in their shaking grasp,
> Pause over half-known faces. All their eyes are ice,
>     But nothing happens.

Owen, then, had discovered the richest seam of his war poetry before he met Sassoon; what the older poet did was to give him the confidence and enthusiasm which drove him onwards to explore it with a sort of poetic fury—'Sweat your guts out writing poetry' was Sassoon's main advice. In a broadcast of 1948,[2] Sassoon gave a succinct account of their

[1] Introduction to anthology *Men Who March Away*, p. 23.
[2] *Wilfred Owen: A Personal Appreciation*, subsequently published in *A Tribute to Wilfred Owen* (compiled T. J. Walsh), 1964, pp. 34–42.

friendship which showed considerable critical insight as well as his usual modesty:

> . . . at that time my critical perceptions were undeveloped, and I was
> slow in realizing that his imagination worked on a larger scale than
> mine, and that in technical accomplishment and intellectual approach
> he was on a higher plane. My trench-sketches were like rockets, sent
> up to illuminate the darkness. They were the first thing of their kind,
> and could claim to be opportune. It was Owen who revealed how, out
> of realistic horror and scorn, poetry might be made.

This is a fair estimate, though it underplays Sassoon's role of encouragement and appreciative criticism, to which Owen himself paid full tribute in his letters. The confidence evident in the exuberant passage set at the head of this chapter manifested itself in the variety and depth of the poet's output between the Craiglockhart meeting and his death. As might be expected, the first effect is direct imitation of Sassoon's style of irony, at the expense of similar targets. In a letter of 22 August 1917 Owen says, '. . . after leaving him, I wrote something in Sassoon's style. This was 'The Dead-beat', an account of a shell-shock case which concludes:

> We sent him down at last, out of the way.
> Unwounded;—stout lad, too, before that strafe.
> Malingering? Stretcher-bearers winked, 'Not half!'
>
> Next day I heard the Doc's well-whiskied laugh:
> 'That scum you sent last night soon died. Hooray.'

This certainly borrows Sassoon's style, but it is not so effective. The speech rhythms of soldiery and doctor are not so happily blended into a poetic medium; the last line, and particularly its final 'Hooray', is overstated. In 'The Letter' Owen essays an entire poem in the vernacular of the trenches:

> With B.E.F. June 10. Dear Wife,
> (O blast this pencil. 'Ere, Bill, lend's a knife.)
> I'm in the pink at present, dear.
> I think the war will end this year.
> We don't see much of them square-'eaded 'Uns. . . .

This lacks the force and discrimination of Sassoon: the soldier's language is not counterpointed by other elements to give it maximum ironic and poetic effect.

Owen's pieces in this vein rarely have the savage economy, the epigrammatic touch of the best of Sassoon. As with his Keatsian strain, it is only when he adds something of himself, that his work is memorable. 'Disabled', for instance, is a superb example of the best effects of Sassoon on Owen. Taking a typical Sassoon theme, Owen grafts a passionate pity on to echoes of his earlier verse-music to achieve a greater remoteness and despair:

> He sat in a wheeled chair, waiting for dark,
> And shivered in his ghastly suit of grey,
> Legless, sewn short at elbow. Through the park
> Voices of boys rang saddening like a hymn,
> Voices of play and pleasure after a day,
> Till gathering sleep had mothered them from him. . . .
>
> Now, he will spend a few sick years in Institutes,
> And do what things the rules consider wise,
> And take whatever pity they may dole.
> To-night he noticed how the women's eyes
> Passed from him to the strong men that were whole.
> How cold and late it is! Why don't they come
> And put him into bed? Why don't they come?

Always when not merely imitating Sassoon, Owen is able to suggest a wider vision and conception. Sassoon channels his disillusion with the Churches' support of the war into the biting satirical caricature of the Bishop; Owen fuses his own lost faith with a more generalized condemnation of what he sees around him:

> Near Golgotha strolls many a priest,
>     And in their faces there is pride
> That they were flesh-marked by the Beast
>     By whom the gentle Christ's denied.

Even in those poems where Sassoon's influence is most obvious, Owen usually suggests a wider conception of the war tragedy than his mentor. The most famous and most effective of these is probably 'Dulce et Decorum Est', where Owen employs the scheme of alternate line rhyming followed by Sassoon in many of his efforts, and the explicit picture of war horror followed by savage satiric conclusion pillorying the civilians at home which is Sassoon's most typical method of constructing a poem. The opening is as vivid as anything of its kind by Sassoon and others:

> Bent double, like old beggars under sacks,
> Knock-kneed, coughing like hags, we cursed through sludge,
> Till on the haunting flares we turned our backs
> And towards our distant rest began to trudge.
> Men marched asleep. Many had lost their boots
> But limped on, blood-shod. All went lame; all blind;
> Drunk with fatigue; deaf even to the hoots
> Of tired, outstripped Five-Nines that dropped behind.

At the end of the description of the gas attack, there is a brief reference to what for Owen was the ultimate horror of war, madness, which threatened in his own nightmares:

> In all my dreams, before my helpless sight,
> He plunges at me, guttering, choking, drowning.

The thought of man's mind helpless under the impact of the new war technology rouses Owen to impressive heights of pity and anger, but the satirical conclusion is a quotation from Horace, casually condemned as 'the old Lie', which characteristically connects the western front and its lessons with civilized experience in other eras:

> If in some smothering dreams you too could pace
> Behind the wagon that we flung him in,
> And watch the white eyes writhing in his face,
> His hanging face, like a devil's sick of sin;
> If you could hear, at every jolt, the blood
> Come gargling from the froth-corrupted lungs,
> Obscene as cancer, bitter as the cud
> Of vile, incurable sores on innocent tongues,—
> My friend, you would not tell with such high zest
> To children ardent for some desperate glory,
> The old Lie: Dulce et decorum est
> Pro patria mori.

In the imagery also, Owen is constantly searching to place the particular experience in the widest possible philosophical context. The superb comparisons of the 'hanging face, like a devil's sick of sin' and the frothing blood which is not only as 'obscene as cancer' but 'bitter as the cud of vile, incurable sores on innocent tongues' suggest a philosophical challenge and outrage as well as the vivid horror of the moment.

'The Send-Off' is apparently a slighter poem, but one whose images linger in the mind long after it has been read, and whose questionings about the morality of war and those who send men to fight it remain relevant more than half a century after the particular war which was its inspiration. The Hardy-like opening of the poem is quieter than the pictures of the front, but just as explicit and as evocative of atmosphere:

> Down the close, darkening lanes they sang their way
> To the siding-shed,
>  And lined the train with faces grimly gay.
>
> Their breasts were stuck all white with wreath and spray
> As men's are, dead.

There is more here than in Sassoon's straightforward contrasts between home and Europe. Though Owen lingers almost affectionately over the details of the picture, he interpolates the uncompromising simile of corpses in the fifth line. By using more complex rhyme and more broken rhythms than Sassoon he increases the impact of this and other effects in the poem, and the directness and simplicity of the language and syntax is nearer to Sorley than Sassoon. The second half of the poem contains no explicit pictures of the conscripts and their various fates, yet achieves a greater impression of remoteness and futility than any other poet achieved on this theme:

> So secretly, like wrongs hushed-up, they went.
> They were not ours:
> We never heard to which front these were sent.
>
> Nor there if they yet mock what women meant
> Who gave them flowers.
>
> Shall they return to beatings of great bells
> In wild train-loads?
> A few, a few, too few for drums and yells,

> May creep back, silent, to still village wells
> Up half-known roads.

The first three lines of this suggest the massive scale of modern warfare and the indifference it engenders: the marvellous opening simile is consolidated by the resolute adherence to monosyllables for the chilling sentiments which form the matter of the next two lines. How far beyond his Keatsian strain has Owen learned to travel, and how effectively!

Even straightforward anger against the civilians and staff far from the front is turned to more constructive philosophic purpose by Owen than by Sassoon, as in the conclusion of 'Insensibility':

> By choice they made themselves immune
> To pity and whatever mourns in man
> Before the last sea and the hapless stars;
> Whatever mourns when many leave these shores;
> Whatever shares
> The eternal reciprocity of tears.

Owen's insistence on pity here brings one inevitably to the famous lines he wrote as part of a planned preface to his war poetry:

> Above all I am not concerned with Poetry.
> My subject is War, and the pity of War.
> The Poetry is in the pity.
> (*Collected Poems*, p. 31)

It would have been conventional to begin this chapter with this quotation rather than with Owen's letter to Sassoon which I chose. The truth is that the statement of a poetic creed as it stands is so crowded with semantic difficulties as to be almost without meaning. Critics have seized on the statement and elaborated it to suit whatever critical view of Owen's work they were projecting. No doubt Owen knew what he meant by the statement and would have elaborated it in due course into something much more definite and with more obvious implications for his work; as it is, his brief notes remain a basis for conjecture rather than the poetic manifesto for which they have often been accepted.

All we can really determine from the preface, or the notes for it which were all Owen was able to pen, is that pity must be the keynote which overrides all else, that troops are not 'flowers for poets' tearful fooling' as he insists elsewhere. But to take as literal Owen's statement that he is 'not concerned with Poetry' would be silly; indeed his most effective work is that which expresses his pity through a mastery of varied poetic effects. Although he declared in a letter to Sassoon that 'I don't want to write anything to which a soldier would say, "No Compris"!' he does not observe this in his best work. Like Wordsworth 'piping simple songs for simple men', Owen finds that his more complex material demands a corresponding complexity and compression of language.

An example of this is Owen's sense of the war as a ritual oblation, which Bergonzi notes in the last year of Owen's work. This is bound to cause some tension when the poet attempts to fuse it with the bitterness and anger which are other elements in his work of this period. Owen's problem of conveying a proper respect for the dead, even in carnage which seems meaningless, is underlined when one considers the earlier verse on this theme, which was still the popular note to sound in 1918. Apart from Brooke's sonnets, the most famous is certainly Laurence Binyon's 'For the Fallen', in which the persuasive solemnity of the four lines later incorporated into the Service of Remembrance should not be allowed to obscure the sonorous banality of the preceding verses:

> Solemn the drums thrill; Death august and royal
> Sings sorrow up into immortal spheres,
> There is music in the midst of desolation
> And a glory that shines upon our tears.
>
> They went with songs to the battle, they were young,
> Straight of limb, true of eye, steady and aglow.
> They were staunch to the end against odds uncounted:
> They fell with their faces to the foe.
>
> They shall grow not old, as we that are left grow old:
> Age shall not weary them, nor the years condemn.
> At the going down of the sun and in the morning
> We will remember them.

Owen's effort to combine dignity with realism, and his own Keatsian strain with the approach encouraged by Sassoon, is seen in the famous sonnet, 'Anthem for Doomed Youth', which seems likely to be as widely anthologised for the next generation as Brooke's 'Soldier' sonnet was for the last. The octet contains some of Owen's best and most characteristic effects:

What passing-bells for these who die as cattle?
  Only the monstrous anger of the guns.
  Only the stuttering rifles' rapid rattle
Can patter out their hasty orisons.
No mockeries now for them; no prayers nor bells,
  Nor any voice of mourning save the choirs,—
The shrill, demented choirs of wailing shells;
  And bugles calling for them from sad shires.

Sound effects and verse-rhythms combine throughout to reinforce exactly the sense of this. There is an air of mastery about the movement from the challenging and uncompromising opening, though the heavy sounds of the second line and the irregular gunfire of the third and fourth to the quieter note of the fifth, which turns out only to be an ironic setting-up for the poem's most remarkable effect, the notion of the wailing shells as a demented choir and the final remoteness of the empty beauty of the bugles recording their deaths at home. Here is a poet who knows what he wishes to do and has all the equipment to bring it off triumphantly. The sestet is perhaps rather less happy:

What candles may be held to speed them all?
  Not in the hands of boys, but in their eyes
Shall shine the holy glimmers of good-byes.
  The pallor of girls' brows shall be their pall;
Their flowers the tenderness of patient minds,
And each slow dusk a drawing-down of blinds.

This is much nearer to reality than Brooke's efforts on similar themes, but Owen has perhaps been beguiled in a similar way by a preoccupation with sound effects. The verse is slacker and less varied than the earlier part of the poem and significantly lacks the compression of ideas and effects so apparent there. The beauty of the sounds disguises the fact that Owen has moved from the anger of the opening into a spurious rationalization of the deaths of 'these who die as cattle' by the externals of grief in those at home. The plangent notes of Owen's threnody here give us a series of effective cadences of which the final couplet is the most remarkable, but the fact that the sonnet is a satisfying construction as word-music cannot disguise the fact that in intellectual development there is an inconsistency.

Owen's most remarkable poem is the fragment entitled 'Strange Meeting' which is sufficient of itself to refute some of the critics who have questioned his steadily growing reputation over the last forty years. The most famous of these is Yeats, who excluded Owen from his compilation of the *Oxford Book of English Verse* in 1936 on the grounds that 'passive suffering is not a proper subject for poetry'. In a letter defending the exclusion to Dorothy Wellesley in December 1936, Yeats described Owen as 'unworthy of the poets' corner of a country newspaper' and his poetry as 'all blood, dirt and sucked sugar-stick'. This is so grotesque as to hint at jealousy, and indeed Owen occasionally suggests the kind of larger effects Yeats was to achieve more consistently in his later verse.

More balanced is the view of John H. Johnston[3] that the war poets in general were too close to the experience to be able to order it coherently in verse. He maintains that even Owen 'does not measure up to the vast tragic potentialities of his material'; only an epic poet could in his view have dealt adequately with the cataclysm. Shorter poems, he thinks, are not suitable vehicles for dealing with the war and its 'vast tragic potentialities'. The number of successful verse epics achieved in any language shows that this medium is an enormously difficult one, but it is surely a mistake in any case to make length a prerequisite for great poetry on any theme. 'Strange Meeting' certainly supports this view, and T. S. Eliot was much more impressed by it than Yeats. He described it as 'a poem which will never be forgotten, and which is not only one of the most moving pieces of verse inspired by the war of 1914–18 but also a technical achievement of great originality'.[4] The technical triumph to which Eliot refers is Owen's use of para-rhyme which is in this poem brought to full fruition.

Professor Johnston suggests that the inspiration for the poem was Sassoon's 'The Rear-Guard', in which a British soldier stumbling through the Hindenburg Line discovers a festering corpse. But this is straightforward realism (a passage from the poem is quoted on page 36). A much more probable source is Sassoon's 'Enemies' which attempts a similar visionary effect:

> He stood alone in some queer sunless place
> Where Armageddon ends. Perhaps he longed
> For days he might have lived; but his young face
> Gazed forth untroubled: and suddenly there thronged

---

[3] *English Poetry of the First World War*, Princeton, 1964.
[4] *A Tribute to Wilfred Owen* (compiled T. J. Walsh), 1964, p. 28.

> Round him the hulking Germans that I shot
> When for his death my brooding rage was hot.

This is worth examination, not to pursue sterile conjectures about Owen's starting-point, but to underline his achievement. Sassoon's techniques and imagery are simply inadequate for this sort of poetic approach and a promising idea remains undeveloped. How much more Owen makes of a similar theme:

> It seemed that out of battle I escaped
> Down some profound dull tunnel, long since scooped
> Through granites which titanic wars had groined.
> Yet also there encumbered sleepers groaned,
> Too fast in thought or death to be bestirred.
> Then, as I probed them, one sprang up, and stared
> With piteous recognition in fixed eyes,
> Lifting distressful hands as if to bless.
> And by his smile, I knew that sullen hall,
> By his dead smile I knew we stood in Hell.
> With a thousand pains that vision's face was grained;
> Yet no blood reached there from the upper ground.

Owen has taken the Keatsian strain of 'Hyperion', adapted it for his own purposes, and grafted on to it the para-rhyme which is seen at its most impressive in the solemn music of this poem, where it creates, as Edmund Blunden says, effects of 'remoteness, darkness, shock, emptiness'.

Perhaps Owen's achievement is a little uneven, reminding us that the poem was still subject to revision at the time of his death. He is either unnecessarily obscure or beguiled by the richness of the sensuous appeal he contrives in this passage:

> I went hunting wild
> After the wildest beauty in the world,
> Which lies not calm in eyes, or braided hair,
> But mocks the steady running of the hour,
> And if it grieves, grieves richlier than here.
> For of my glee might many men have laughed,
> And of my weeping something had been left,
> Which must die now.

In a later couplet the nouns could be interchanged without noticeable alteration of the sense:

> Courage was mine, and I had mystery,
> Wisdom was mine, and I had mastery.

But considering the ambitious nature of what he is attempting, Owen is for the most part impressively successful, and the poem is at once the consummation of his own work and a foreshadowing of the poetic approach which was to dominate the next two decades. It is ironic that Yeats should emerge as so vehement a critic of Owen, for the most visionary and prophetic lines of the poem foreshadow some of Yeats' own later work:[5]

> Now men will go content with what we spoiled,
> Or, discontent, boil bloody, and be spilled.
> They will be swift with swiftness of the tigress.
> None will break ranks, though nations trek from progress.

Some of the images fuse the material of Owen's very real nightmares with a much wider suggestion in a way which Eliot and Yeats were to develop into a characteristic strain of Twentieth Century poetry.

> Foreheads of men have bled where no wounds were

is a striking compression of this sort, achieving at once the horrific and striking visual effect of an imagist painting, the suggestion of the madness which for Owen is always war's ultimate horror, and the vaguer idea of civilized thought itself being cast into jeopardy by the war.

The poem closes with lines which show in their dying fall and changes of rhythm Owen's mastery of his medium and of the scheme of his poem; they also read like an epitaph on the poetry of the war and the attitudes of the soldiery. To Sorley's attitude towards the foe and Sassoon's use of specific incident Owen adds his own power over effects of sound and rhythm to suggest weariness and hopelessness, and to transmute the particular deaths into a larger context:

> I am the enemy you killed, my friend.
> I knew you in this dark: for so you frowned
> Yesterday through me as you jabbed and killed.
> I parried; but my hands were loath and cold.
> Let us sleep now. . . .

[5] E.g. 'The Second Coming', 1921.

# 5. Isaac Rosenberg:
## Odd Man Out

I never joined the army from patriotic reasons. Nothing can justify
war. I suppose we must all fight to get the trouble over. Anyhow
before the war I helped at home when I could and I did other things
which helped to keep things going. I thought if I'd join there would be
the separation allowance for my mother. . . .

(*Collected Works of Isaac Rosenberg*)

The low-key uncertainty of Rosenberg in his letters provides a consistent
contrast with the large-scale effects he aimed at in his verse. The above
passage from a letter to Edward Marsh late in 1915 underlines the
difference in background between Rosenberg and the other major poets
of the Great War.

Rosenberg's life was a continuing history of disappointment and
anticlimax; his obscure death at the age of twenty-seven on All Fools
Day, 1 April 1918, lost with all members of a night patrol and with his
body never found, seemed a fitting culmination of a sad chronicle of
small failures. The steady advance of his reputation over the last forty
years has brought some of the success Rosenberg so earnestly desired and
was so consistently denied during his lifetime. Many of the virtues now
noted in his poetry, such as his stubborn quest for individuality which
made him avoid convention at all costs, were the qualities which
confined him to a narrow audience at the time of his writing.

Rosenberg was born on 25 November 1890, of Russian Jewish
immigrants. Mainly it seems from a determination to secure some sort of
education for the children, the family moved into the teeming East End
Jewish community in 1897; Isaac was educated at Jewish elementary
schools in Stepney until he left school at barely fourteen at the end of
1904. After unhappy years in which he struggled with the unpleasant

drudgery of an engraver's workshop, he secured patronage which enabled him to study at the Slade from October 1911 to March 1914. Rosenberg spent the period from June 1914 to May 1915 in South Africa at his sister's house. He enlisted in the Suffolk Bantams regiment at the end of October 1915; apparently pessimism at his lack of success and chronic poverty overcame his indecisive pacifism in the manner suggested in the letter quoted above.

Throughout the pre-war period Rosenberg was uncertain whether he should devote himself to poetry or to the visual arts, and the tension probably partly accounts for the slenderness of his output at the Slade. As early as 1912 he wrote to Laurence Binyon that 'I find writing interferes with my drawing a good deal and is far more exhausting.'[1]

While the Georgian 'renaissance' was in full swing in 1913, Rosenberg produced little of consequence in painting or poetry. In 1912 he had published 50 of his early poems in *Night and Day and Other Poems*; the work is ineffective save for occasional flashes and is interesting chiefly for its markedly Blakean influence. Only 22 of Rosenberg's total output of 230 poems are war poems, and of these some are inchoate or fragmentary; yet his war output marks the climax of his work and is the surest evidence of the major poetic figure whose emergence was so abruptly cut short. The pre-war poetry shows Rosenberg working out for himself, with many false starts and continuous struggle, the individual voice in which he felt sure he must speak. It shows first the influence of and then a rejection of the Romantics as he recognizes his need for something more rough and sinewy. By 1914 the imagist influence is apparent in his work, but he is characteristically not won over to it entirely. He read Marsh's first volume of Georgian Poetry early in 1915; he was particularly impressed by these poets' 'personal vision' and simplicity of expression, two qualities which he felt himself to be striving for, but the pastoral nostalgia which formed the basis of the movement was totally outside his experience and had no attraction for him. The truth is that while Rosenberg was interested in all the major artistic movements of the pre-war period, he was too resolute and stubborn an individualist to give his allegiance wholly to any of them.

This is easily illustrated by his first reaction to the war:

[1] M. de Sausmarez, *The Drawings and Paintings of Isaac Rosenberg*, p. 28.

On Receiving News of the War
(Cape Town, 1914)

Snow is a strange white word.
No ice or frost
Has asked of bud or bird
For Winter's cost.

Yet ice and frost and snow
From earth to sky
This Summer land doth know.
No man knows why. . . .

O! ancient crimson curse!
Corrode, consume.
Give back this universe
Its pristine bloom.

This monosyllabic directness marks a more sober and chilling apprehension of the approaching holocaust than any other poet achieved. Despite the hope for regenerative effects expressed in the last stanza, war is not the crusade of 'swimmers into cleanness leaping' as it was seen by Brooke and by others who were later to learn better; it is an 'ancient crimson curse'. This striving to place the horrors of this particular war in a much more generalized context of history is to be characteristic of Rosenberg even when confronted with the immediate horrors of the trenches in due course. Only Owen sometimes aims at similar effects, and he does not achieve them all with the consistency which Rosenberg secures. The imagist's use of ice and frost and snow in the first two stanzas of the poem above is worked through with consistency. Rosenberg's manipulation of the multiple association of his images, with each capable of interpretation both for immediate effect and in a larger framework, is characteristic of his best poetry: it is when he fails to control these associations fully that his work lapses into obscurity or incoherence. His other poem dealing with the outbreak of the war, 'August 1914', was actually written in spring 1916, but shows the same complex use of striking images:

Three lives hath one life—
Iron, honey, gold.

> The gold, the honey gone—
> Left is the hard and cold.
>
> Iron are our lives
> Molten right through our youth.
> A burnt space through ripe fields
> A fair mouth's broken tooth.

Rosenberg is distinguished from the other major war poets by his Jewish background, and the sense of a culture and a historical perspective which transcend national boundaries is always an element in his verse. Even when his resilience to the trench experience was at its lowest, the ancient sorrows and hopes of Hebraism are active, as in his last poem, sent to Marsh two days before his final, fatal night patrol:

> Through these pale cold days
> What dark faces burn
> Out of three thousand years,
> And their wild eyes yearn,
> While underneath their brows
> Like waifs their spirits grope
> For the pools of Hebron again—
> For Lebanon's summer slope.

Rosenberg was different also in his urban, working-class background. It has already been remarked that this meant he had no English pastoral nostalgia to set as a contrast against front-line experience. More immediately and more importantly, it meant that he experienced the war as a private, with all the extra suffering that this entailed. With his frail physique, congenital forgetfulness and intellectual preoccupations, few men could have been less fitted for the experience than Rosenberg. No wonder he wrote that, 'The army is the most detestable invention on this earth and no-one but a private in the army knows what it is to be a slave.' Nor was there much respite for him. From the moment when he reached the front in the summer of 1916 until his death, Rosenberg spent the twenty months in or near the trenches save for two brief periods. The strain involved is indicated by the fact that Owen's trench experience, despite its intense effect upon his mind and work, amounted to only five months, and that as an officer. Rosenberg's determination to protect his inner life as a poet and his intermittent contacts with Marsh and others by letter were his only sustenance in his darkest moments.

At one such moment in 1916, Rosenberg's spirits were raised by a letter from Lascelles Abercrombie which contained the most perceptive evaluation of his work up to that date: 'A good many of your poems strike me as experimental and not quite certain of themselves. But on the other hand I always find a vivid and original impulse; and what I like most in your songs is your power to make the concealed poetic power in words come flashing out. Some of your phrases are remarkable; no one who writes poetry could help envying some of them.'[2] The comment refers almost exclusively to Rosenberg's pre-war verse: he was encouraged by it to concentrate on making 'the concealed poetic power in words come flashing out' more consistently. Where isolated lines had blazed with a fierce intensity, Rosenberg in his finest war poems obtained more sustained effects.

The first manifestation of this consistency is 'Marching (As seen from the Left File)'. The first stanza allies the painter's eye for colour effects to a rhythm designed to emphasize the tramp of men:

> My eyes catch ruddy necks
> Sturdily pressed back—
> All a red brick moving glint.
> Like flaming pendulums, hands
> Swing across the khaki—
> Mustard-coloured khaki—
> To the automatic feet.

The second stanza generalizes the theme and changes the poetic method; a rapid series of metaphors packed with complex associations first emphasizes the recurring nature of war through the centuries and then the new, impersonal, machine-like horror of modern mass-warfare. The poem concludes with one of those memorable phrases to which Abercrombie had referred, which this time forms a fitting conclusion to what has gone before rather than blazing in splendid isolation:

> We husband the ancient glory
> In these bared necks and hands,
> Not broke is the forge of Mars;

[2] Quoted in *Journey to the Trenches*, J. Cohen, p. 130.

> But a subtler brain beats iron
> To shoe the hoofs of death
> (Who paws dynamic air now).
> Blind fingers loose an iron cloud
> To rain immortal darkness
> On strong eyes.

In the sixteen lines of 'Returning, We Hear the Larks' Rosenberg again achieves a rich compression of effects. The opening places the scene and the attitudes with considerable economy:

> Sombre the night is.
> And though we have our lives, we know
> What sinister threat lurks there.
>
> Dragging these anguished limbs, we only know
> This poison-blasted track opens on our camp—
> On a little safe sleep.

Rosenberg then introduces the incongruous beauty of the larks' song in the night, startling in its effect on men starved of such music. Other poets, such as Graves and Blunden, noted the irony of nature's beauties enduring obstinately amidst the battle, but they were content to underline the irony. Rosenberg, characteristically, searches further than this into the experience. Arguing with Marsh in a letter, he explained of his poetry, 'I don't think there should be any vagueness at all; but a sense of something hidden and felt to be there.' It is in just such an attempt to evoke all the elements of an experience that he uses similes for the larks' song which emphasize the precarious and even dangerous quality of this music in such a setting:

> But hark! joy—joy—strange joy.
> Lo! heights of night ringing with unseen larks.
> Music showering on our upturned list'ning faces.
>
> Death could drop from the dark
> As easily as song—
> But song only dropped,
> Like a blind man's dreams on the sand
> By dangerous tides,

> Like a girl's dark hair for she dreams no
>     ruin lies there,
> Or her kisses where a serpent hides.

The uneasy beauty of the moment is emphasized by images which are themselves uneasy, and more effective in being culled from experience outside the war itself. Amazingly, Rosenberg succeeds in at once pinpointing a moment in the war itself and suggesting the fragile and sometimes illusory quality of beauty in the human condition in general.

Rosenberg can capture the daily squalor and suffering of the private's war in the trenches as well as any of the war poets, but he is detached enough to see it first and foremost as rich poetic material. He was a poet and artist long before he reached the front and determined to use his experiences there to further his development: an aesthetic rather than a social purpose dominates his approach. In his capacity to stand away from the experience and convey it with strictly controlled emotion, at times even with an apparent absence of emotion, he is unique among the war poets.

In his own reading in the immediate pre-war period he had discovered and been much influenced by the metaphysical poets: Donne is as important an influence for him as Keats is for Owen. Not surprisingly in view of this, he embraces as material the trench soldier's daily curse, lice. His first attempt, 'The Immortals', does little more than convey the nightmarish anger and frustration they arouse, but by February 1917, he has abandoned straightforward irony for something much more original in 'Louse Hunting'. Rosenberg observes with a painter's eye, then transfixes the form and colour in words to capture a grotesque arabesque:

> Nudes—stark and glistening,
> Yelling in lurid glee. Grinning faces
> And raging limbs
> Whirl over the floor on fire;
> For a shirt verminously busy
> Yon soldier tore from his throat
> With oaths
> Godhead might shrink at, but not the lice.
> And soon the shirt was aflare
> Over the candle he'd lit while we lay.

Whereas others would have pointed the misery and pity of the soldier's
lot, Rosenberg resolutely avoids any overt acknowledgement of this:

> Then we all sprang up and stript
> To hunt the verminous brood.
> Soon like a demon's pantomime
> The place was raging.
> See the silhouettes agape,
> See the gibbering shadows
> Mixed with the baffled arms on the wall.
> See gargantuan hooked fingers
> Pluck in supreme flesh
> To smutch supreme littleness.
> See the merry limbs in hot Highland fling
> Because some wizard vermin
> Charmed from the quiet this revel
> When our ears were half lulled
> By the dark music
> Blown from Sleep's trumpet.

The painter's apprehension of the details of the scene is underlined by the
poet's perception of ironic contrasts. The metaphysical paradox of the
'supreme flesh' plagued by 'supreme littleness' is given additional vigour
by the artist's hyperbole of the 'gargantuan hooked fingers' glimpsed by
the shirt's flame. The fierce animal energy which is the nightmarish
reality is set against the 'dark music' of sleep, a final image by which
Rosenberg again leaves us with a feeling of a wider doom surrounding
even so explicit a picture as this. The effect is that of the frozen music of
sculpture, and the lines recall Sassoon's comments in his introduction to
Rosenberg's collected poems in 1949 on the sculptural quality of
Rosenberg's method: ' . . . he *modelled* words with fierce energy and
aspiration, finding ecstasy in form, dreaming in grandeurs of superb light
and deep shadow; his poetic visions are mostly in sombre colours and
looming sculptural masses, molten and amply wrought.'

Another poem of Rosenberg's which uses a characteristically
metaphysical starting point for a commentary on contemporary horrors
is the well-known 'Break of Day in the Trenches', written in the late
summer of 1916. This has many virtues, some akin to those of the best of
his fellow war poets, some peculiar to Rosenberg's genius alone. The

poem begins from the view that the men in the opposing lines of trenches
are not enemies but common victims of this peculiar hell. To realize half a
century later the individuality of thought as well as of expression in this
poem one must recall the kind of writing prevalent at the time. A month
or two after Rosenberg wrote this poem Bruce Bairnsfather was penning
in *Bullets and Billets* to be published in December 1916, this account of the
unrehearsed meeting of British and German soldiers during the unofficial
trench truce of Christmas 1915:

> The shortest effect I can give of the impression I had was that our men,
> superior, broadminded, more frank, and lovable beings, were
> regarding these faded, unimaginative products of perverted Kultur as a
> set of objectionable but amusing lunatics whose heads had *got* to be
> eventually smacked.

Rosenberg's unforced lines make a sharp contrast; there is no sign that he
was intensely angered by the kind of writing fed to the civilians at home,
as Sassoon and Owen so markedly were. He is simply uninterested in it,
and reaction to it is not the material of poetry for him; he is interested
only in securing the central poetic effect of his theme:

> The darkness crumbles away—
> It is the same old druid Time as ever.
> Only a live thing leaps my hand—
> A queer sardonic rat—
> As I pull the parapet's poppy
> To stick behind my ear.
> Droll rat, they would shoot you if they knew
> Your cosmopolitan sympathies.
> Now you have touched this English hand
> You will do the same to a German—
> Soon, no doubt, if it be your pleasure
> To cross the sleeping green between.
> (*Break of Day in the Trenches*)

As usual, Rosenberg is concerned to place the war in a wider context. The
generality of the eternal elements of darkness and time is followed by a
very specific detail of this particular war: it is an effective poetic device
which he often uses. Rosenberg's originality is marked by the use he
makes of the rat here. Many poets mention the rats as part of the

incidental, peripheral horrors of trench life. Only Rosenberg uses the rat as a device to convey a complex intellectual idea: the tragic irony that this low scavenger is better fitted for life at the front than the lords of creation:

> It seems you inwardly grin as you pass
> Strong eyes, fine limbs, haughty athletes
> Less chanced than you for life,
> Bonds to the whims of murder,
> Sprawled in the bowels of the earth,
> The torn fields of France.

In returning at the close of the poem to the poppy he had pulled at the beginning, Rosenberg characteristically attempts to suggest the wider implications of this moment of experience in lines that are deliberately ambivalent:

> Poppies whose roots are in man's veins
> Drop, and are ever dropping;
> But mine in my ear is safe,
> Just a little white with the dust.

The fine image of the first of these lines refers of course to the fact that poppies are by this time literally rooting in the bodies of the dead, an association which enables Rosenberg to suggest in the next line that men may drop just as easily as this most transient of flowers. Equally, there is a hint in the last two lines that man and poppy may fall together; the deliberate pathos of the last line, ending as it does with the word 'dust' with its myriad associations, suggests the uncertainty of the soldier's hold on life.

Rosenberg's attempts to develop his most striking images into a form of symbolism mark him as the most ambitious of the war poets and as a forerunner of the poetic developments of the twenties and thirties. The attempt is consistently successful in only a few of his poems, most of which have now been referred to, and elsewhere it sometimes leads to obscurity and apparently meaningless complexity. Thus 'Daughters of War', an ambitious poem which he thought his best to date when writing to Marsh on 30 July 1917, is only fitfully successful because its intellectual framework is not convincingly worked out in terms of imagery. Even some of his shorter poems are not so consistent in tone and verse-effects as those quoted above.

Unquestionably Rosenberg's finest poem, and one which many modern commentators would place ahead of Owen's 'Strange Meeting' as the greatest poem to come out of the war, is 'Dead Man's Dump'. Where 'Daughters of War' attempted to be wholly symbolic, 'Dead Man's Dump' continually counterpoints realism and symbolism in a manner which by now emerges as characteristic of the poet's best work. V. de S. Pinto noted in Rosenberg an apocalyptic vision of the horror of modern warfare comparable with that of Owen. Certainly that is most apparent in 'Dead Man's Dump', but Rosenberg makes a different, more detached, yet even more intense use of that vision than does Owen.

The poem begins with an explicit picture, but Rosenberg fuses realism with symbolism by using images which have wide suggestions:

> The plunging limbers over the shattered track
> Racketed with their rusty freight,
> Stuck out like many crowns of thorns,
> And the rusty stakes like sceptres old
> To stay the flood of brutish men
> Upon our brothers dear.

The crown of thorns is a precisely effective visual image for the rusty barbed wire, but by its rich associations immediately places the moment so vividly evoked in the first two lines in a context of two thousand years of Christian culture; similarly the reference to sceptres attempting to stay the flood recalls Canute's ineffective attempts to stay the sea's flood and suggests the present wiring operations will be equally fruitless.

As usual, Rosenberg is seeking to concern himself and his readers not with particular deaths but with an exploration of death in general. He describes the specific dead who are his starting point in deliberately impersonal and unemotional terms:

> The wheels lurched over sprawled dead
> But pained them not, though their bones crunched,
> Their shut mouths made no moan.
> They lie there huddled, friend and foeman,
> Man born of man, and born of woman,
> And shells go crying over them
> From night till night and now.

Rosenberg now develops the idea which he has outlined in 'Break of Day

in the Trenches' and 'Daughters of War', that the culmination of the
relationship between man and nature arrives when the bodies of the dead
return to the soil:

> Earth has waited for them,
> All the time of their growth
> Fretting for their decay:
> Now she has them at last!
> In the strength of their strength
> Suspended—stopped and held.

John H. Johnston has noted a curious division in Rosenberg's work
between the timeless, visionary mode, most obviously instanced in
'Daughters of War', and the mode which is based on the immediately
realized sensous experience, as in 'Returning, We Hear the Larks'. The
modes are brought together in this poem, though Johnston considers that
the elements do not merge into a satisfactory artistic whole; he finds the
poem a succession of brilliant lyric fragments. This seems less than fair:
though one has to accept different styles in different sections of the 13
irregular stanzas, which vary from 2 to 9 lines in length, it is always
obvious why Rosenberg is switching styles and moving from the
particular to the general and back again. In the generalized sections about
death the imagery is sometimes of haunting and evocative brilliance:

> None saw their spirits' shadow shake the grass,
> Or stood aside for the half used life to pass
> Out of those doomed nostrils and the doomed mouth,
> When the swift iron burning bee
> Drained the wild honey of their youth.

The starting-point of this is not the moral condemnation or the pity of the
death, as in Owen's 'Anthem for Doomed Youth' but the death itself: the
concept is so much more ambitious and in this passage so brilliantly
realized that Owen's sonnet appears superficial by comparison.

One would concede that the vaguest section of the poem which
follows these lines, where Rosenberg strives to explore the concept of
death itself, is the least successful. But as soon as he returns to the by now
familiar method of using a particular incident as a springboard into wider
considerations and more associative imagery, he achieves one of the most
impressive passages of this or any other war poem:

> A man's brains splattered on
> A stretcher-bearer's face;
> His shook shoulders slipped their load,
> But when they bent to look again
> The drowning soul was sunk too deep
> For human tenderness.
>
> They left this dead with the older dead,
> Stretched at the cross roads.
>
> Burnt black by strange decay
> Their sinister faces lie,
> The lid over each eye,
> The grass and coloured clay
> More motion have than they,
> Joined to the great sunk silences.

Again the specific detail of the dead is consolidated into something which transcends mere anger or pity by the addition of the superb and effortless last line of this, perhaps the finest of Rosenberg's great phrases.

The poem closes with a death which unites the anguish of the living and dead as the stretcher-bearers arrive too late to help the stricken man, who is used as a universalized symbol of death in war as well as an individual:

> Here is one not long dead;
> His dark hearing caught our far wheels,
> And the choked soul stretched weak hands
> To reach the living word the far wheels said,
> The blood-dazed intelligence beating for light,
> Crying through the suspense of the far torturing wheels
> Swift for the end to break
> Or the wheels to break,
> Cried as the tide of the world broke over his sight.
>
> Will they come? Will they ever come?
> Even as the mixed hoofs of the mules,
> The quivering-bellied mules,
> And the rushing wheels all mixed
> With his tortured upturned sight.
> So we crashed round the bend,

We heard his weak scream,
We heard his very last sound,
And our wheels grazed his dead face.

The bleak power of this derives from Rosenberg's capacity to realize a
deeply felt experience with an intense but detached poetic vision,
without overt moral comment. It is this capacity which dominates all his
best work.

Towards the end of 1916 he wrote to Laurence Binyon ' . . . I am
determined that this war, with all its powers for devastation, shall not
master my poeting; that is, if I am lucky enough to come through all
right. I will not leave a corner of my consciousness covered up, but
saturate myself with the strange and extraordinary new conditions of this
life, and it will all refine itself into poetry later on.' He did not of course
'come through' and there was no opportunity for the experience to
'refine itself'. Even 'Dead Man's Dump' is unrevised and Rosenberg's
modest verdict in sending it to Marsh was 'I don't think what I've
written is very good but I think the substance is, and when I work on it
I'll make it fine.' But his courage and determination to continue writing
in seemingly impossible conditions brought its triumph in the few
marvellous poems on which his claim to immortality seems each year
more securely based.

# Select Bibliography

The extracts in the text have been taken from the following editions:

Rupert Brooke: *The Poetical Works of Rupert Brooke*, ed. G. Keynes, Faber and Faber, 1963.

*The Prose of Rupert Brooke*, ed. C. Hassall, Sidgwick and Jackson, 1956.

Charles Sorley: *Marlborough and Other Poems*, Cambridge University Press, 1916.

*The Letters of Charles Sorley*, 1919.

Siegfried Sassoon: *Collected Poems, 1908–1956*, Faber and Faber, 1961.

*Siegfried's Journey, 1916–1920,* Faber and Faber, 1945.

Wilfred Owen: *The Collected Poems of Wilfred Owen*, ed. C. Day Lewis Chatto and Windus, 1963.

*Collected Letters*, ed. H. Owen and J. Bell, Oxford University Press 1967.

Isaac Rosenberg: *The Collected Poems of Isaac Rosenberg*, ed. G. Bottomley and D. Harding, Chatto and Windus, 1974.

*The Collected Works of Isaac Rosenberg*, ed. G. Bottomley and D Harding, 1937.

Robert Graves: *Goodbye to All That*, Penguin, 1957.

*Georgian Poetry* (selected James Reeves), Penguin, 1962.

Bruce Bairnsfather: *Bullets and Billets*, 1916.

Laurence Binyon, Julian Grenfell, Ivor Gurney, Henry Newbolt, Eden Philpott and William Watson: *Poetry of the First World War*, ed. M Hussey, Longman, 1967.

For further reading the student is referred to the following:

Bergonzi, Bernard, *Heroes' Twilight*, Constable, 1965.

Blunden, Edmund, *War Poets 1914–18* (Writers and their Work, No 100) Longman, 1958.

Blunden, Edmund, Memoir at beginning of *The Poems of Wilfred Owen*, Chatto and Windus, 1960.

Cohen, Joseph, *Journey to the Trenches*, Robson Books, 1975.

Ford, Boris, ed., *Pelican Guide to English Literature*, Vol. 7, Penguin, 1973.

Hassall, Christopher, *Rupert Brooke*, Faber and Faber, 1964.

Johnston, John H., *English Poetry of the First World War*, Princeton University Press, 1964.

Liddiard, Jean, *Isaac Rosenberg: The Half Used Life*, Gollancz, 1975.

Owen, Harold, *Journey from Obscurity* (3 volumes), Oxford University Press, 1963, 1964, 1965.

Pinto, V. de S., *Crisis in English Poetry, 1880–1940*, Hutchinson, 1951

Silkin, Jon, *Out of Battle: The Poetry of the Great War*, Oxford University Press, 1972.

Stallworthy, Jon, *Wilfred Owen* (Chatterton Lecture to British Academy, 1970), Oxford University Press, 1971.

Stallworthy, Jon, *Poets of the First World War*, Oxford University Press (with Imperial War Museum), 1975.

Thorpe, Michael, *Siegfried Sassoon: A Critical Study*, University of Leiden, 1966.

Welland, D. S. R., *Wilfred Owen: A Critical Study*, Chatto and Windus, 1960.

Wilson, Jean Moorcroft, *Isaac Rosenberg, Poet and Painter*, Cecil Woolf, 1975.

*Anthologies*

Black, E. L., ed., *1914–18 in Poetry*, University of London Press, 1970.

Gardner, Brian, ed., *Up the Line to Death: The War Poets 1914–18*, Methuen, 1964.

Parsons, I. M., ed., *Men who March Away: Poems of the First World War*, Chatto and Windus, 1968.

# Index